THINGS TO COME

AN ILLUSTRATED HISTORY
OF THE
SCIENCE FICTION FILM

THINGS TO COME

AN ILLUSTRATED HISTORY OF THE SCIENCE FICTION FILM

By

DOUGLAS MENVILLE
and R. REGINALD

INTRODUCTION BY RAY BRADBURY

NYT

Times
BOOKS

THINGS TO COME:
AN ILLUSTRATED HISTORY OF THE SCIENCE FICTION FILM

Copyright © 1977 by R. Reginald and Douglas Menville.
For information, address: Times Books, a division of Quadrangle/The New York Times Book Co., Inc., Three Park Avenue, New York, N.Y. 10016. Manufactured in the United States of America. Published simultaneously in Canada by Fitzhenry & Whiteside Ltd., Toronto.

International Standard Book Number:
    0-8129-0710-8 (hardbound)
    0-8129-6287-7 (paperbound)

Library of Congress Catalog Card Number: 77-79033

First Edition—November, 1977

Produced and designed by R. Reginald, The Borgo Press, San Bernardino, California. Typesetting and paste-up by Holly Sullivan. Cover design by Beth Tondreau.

The authors wish to thank the following film companies for permission to reproduce the stills and pictures used in this book: Metro-Goldwyn-Mayer, Paramount Pictures, United Artists, Walt Disney Studios, Twentieth Century-Fox, Warner Brothers, Allied Artists, Hammer Films, Columbia Pictures, American International Pictures, Argos, Toho, Embassy, Realart, Cinerama, Rank Film Distributors, Icarus, Les Films Armorial, Graffitti, USA, British Lion, RKO, Eagle-Lion, Lippert, Republic. Any omissions from this list are unintentional.

Miscellaneous photo credits:

Title Page: **Things to Come** (London Films, 1936)
Contents Page: **Things to Come** (London Films, 1936)
Page 1: Maria the robot, from **Metropolis** (Ufa, 1926)
Page 39: The futuristic city of **Just Imagine** (Fox, 1930)
Page 77: Gort the robot and his alien master Klaatu (Michael Rennie), from **The Day the Earth Stood Still** (Twentieth Century-Fox, 1951)
Page 115: Man takes a step into space, in **2001: A Space Odyssey** (MGM, 1968)
Page 159: The '''droids'' from **Star Wars** (Twentieth Century-Fox, 1977): C3PO and R2-D2

This book is
respectfully
dedicated to:

Georges Melies
Fritz Lang
Boris Karloff
Willis O'Brien
Buster Crabbe
Sir Alexander Korda
William Cameron Menzies
George Pal
Robert Wise
Ray Harryhausen
Stanley Kubrick
and
George Lucas

—the greatest.

The past is but the beginning of a beginning, and all that is and has been is but the twilight of the dawn...A day will come when beings who are now latent in our thoughts and hidden in our loins shall stand upon this earth as one stands upon a footstool, and shall laugh and reach out their hands amid the stars.

—H. G. Wells

CONTENTS

INTRODUCTION

It is good that this book has been written, so as to remind us of how far back the history of science fiction films goes. When you think of films and science fiction you think of Melies and you think of beginnings. It seems we fanatic futurists have always been around, always under cosmic foot, always saying, years later: I told you so.

I don't say it will, but a book like this COULD make us aware of the fact that a huge lot of science fiction goes on under our lip and no one speaks its name.

Pure SF aside, when was the last time you heard anyone describe **Singing in the Rain** as a science fiction film?

You heard it first HERE.

And it IS, you know, though you won't find it listed or analyzed in this book.

How else describe the advent of an impossible technology that knocked an industry endwise and resulted in a flood of Englishmen invading Santa Barbara to live forever and work in flicks? If I had been alive in 1918 and written such a script, about films one day 'enunciating,' speaking in tongues, you would have laughed me up the aisle and out the exit. Clap-trap, you would have cried, which is another way of saying SF. Yet sound DID arrive. And its history is told in an ''invisible'' SF film with Gene Kelly and Donald O'Connor.

Or, again, and again the film isn't found in this book, when did you hear your last discussion of **Lawrence of Arabia** as son of Gernsbach, nephew to Wells and Verne?

You heard it first here.

For central to the plot of Lawrence is Old fading, New arriving. New means machines, freshly invented, not as yet fully tried. Lawrence warns the Arab chiefs to pull back. Metal and fabric demons will fill the skies and drop fire and death, he says, move your tents, disperse your camels and horses. The Arabs give him that disdainful look that only camels and owners of camels can give. The next instant, a fleet of biplanes fall out of the sun and unravel the tents and the sanity of desert kings.

Science fiction.

If I had written this story in 1900 you would have cried out balderdash, yet another synonym for the fiction that tests today's ignorance against tomorrow's surprises.

You can make a game of it. Look back on the films you've seen the past ten years, or the TV shows, and figure which were SF but you were too sleepy to notice. **The Avengers**, for one, was SF every week, week after week, year on year. All hail, Steed and Peel. **Mission Impossible**, more often than not, the same.

But enough. I was merely testing to make sure you were awake now, as you prepare to journey with this book from Melies to Lang to Pal to Kubrick to Lucas. It is a fascinating history, full of too much Moon garbage and not enough tail of the Great Comet, some of it glorious in its insanity, some of it stunning in its comprehension of the needs of man's soul.

All along the way you will find our hunger to know and survive the knowing. The touchstone reared and left on earth in **2001** is kin to the man and the words spoken at the end of Wells's uneven but still magnificent **Things to Come**. ''Which shall it be? Which SHALL it be?'' is asked by both. The stars or the dust of the grave? The stars! says Cabal. BEYOND the stars, says the great knowledge-giving monument which casts its sublime shadow across Kubrick's dream.

The descriptions of each film herein seem to the point, to me, accurately and succinctly laid out. Plus, the rating of each film, measuring each against the wall to see how tall it stands, seems fair and much to my own taste. There will be differences, of course. Some of you may find **Things to Come** to be the ultimate bore, while giving higher marks to inadvertent laugh riots like **Planet of the Apes**. Faced with this, our authors have come out more than remarkably well.

Reading this book may well prepare you for your next session at the television set where some vague ghost of a new idea may ring an echo. You will probably find it in these pages, haunting the **Black Lagoon** or harvesting the deeps with James Mason's Captain Nemo.

It's a good read, all the way. I put it aside only to ask you this:

When was the last time someone told you that **The Magnificent Ambersons** was science-fiction?

Figure THAT one out!

And don't write to me. Write to the editors and make their lives miserable.

RAY BRADBURY
Los Angeles, Calif.
July 26th, 1977

FOREWORD

The science fiction film is eighty years old this year (1977), and it seems appropriate that we celebrate this anniversary with a full-length history. A Frenchman named Georges Melies is generally credited with making the first SF film, **A Trip to the Moon** (also issued under several other titles), released in France during 1902. Melies was quite popular in his day, and his fantastic features were sufficiently successful to prompt other filmmakers in France, Germany, and Britain to try these unusual themes. These early silent shorts developed in two ways, towards multi-chapter serials having as many as sixty episodes, and then into the full-length features familiar to modern audiences. The first great classic of science fiction cinema was Fritz Lang's **Metropolis**, released in Germany in 1926. Lang's second SF film, **Die Frau im Mond** (1929), was also one of the last of the silents, as movie technology continued to develop at a rapid pace.

H. G. Wells wrote the script for the second "big" science fiction picture, **Things to Come** (1936), a strange combination of Wellsian pessimism (including a thirty-year version of World War II) and utopianism (science triumphs over the destructive powers of mankind in the 21st century). The next fourteen years were a fallow period for SF cinema, as the genre virtually disappeared as an identifiable category from movie theatres. By 1950, the post-war boom in science fiction literature was beginning to gather steam, and Robert Heinlein's classic novel, **Rocket Ship Galileo**, filmed as **Destination Moon**, was enough of a cinematic success that filmmakers everywhere began turning to science fiction as a profitable "B" category, much like the Western genre. In the late 1950s, the SF film degenerated into a seemingly unending series of monster flicks, flying saucer movies, and creature-from-outer-space pictures. Fortunately, most of these tiresome and over-worked strains eventually died out; beginning with **The Time Machine** (1960), good science fiction movies began appearing at theatres once again.

Two films changed the SF world irrevocably. **2001: A Space Odyssey** (1968), Stanley Kubrick's adaptation of Arthur C. Clarke's story, was the first science fiction blockbuster, the first SF picture to challenge the minds and dazzle the eyes of a wide general audience. **2001** was a stunning spectacle, a cold, stark, technically impressive visual poem to the beauty and wonder of outer space. More importantly, **2001** was an enormous financial success, doubling a $10 million investment, and demonstrating, once and for all, that there was indeed a market for well-made, large-budget SF films. But **2001** was not the perfect SF picture, having a certain disjunction in story line that obscured the plot, and made it difficult for the ordinary viewer to follow the action. **2001** sold on the basis of its visual effects, which were far superior to anything else put on the screen prior to that time. The future had finally arrived on the screen.

It took filmmakers a very long time to exceed the power of **2001**. In the next nine years, such films as **THX 1138**, **A Clockwork Orange** (Kubrick's new film), **Slaughterhouse-Five**, **A Boy and His Dog**, **Logan's Run**, **The Man Who Fell to Earth**, **Silent Running**, **The Last Days of Man on Earth** achieved an overall standard of excellence seldom seen in early fantastic cinema. And **Zardoz** (1974), a magnificent visual parable of life and death, remains one of the two or three best SF films ever made. Unfortunately, none of these films had the impact of **2001**, because none did as well commercially. **Zardoz** may well be a better picture than **2001**, both visually and conceptually; but **Zardoz** did poorly at the box-office, and was largely overlooked in consequence. The perfect SF film had yet to be made.

George Lucas's **Star Wars** (1977) may well become the top-grossing motion picture of all time, an astonishing position for a blatantly science-fictional film. Called by **Time** magazine "the year's best film," **Star Wars** is clearly in a class by itself: in the entire history of SF cinema, there has never been anything to equal the incredible vitality and sense of wonder that permeates the film. This is partially due to advances in special effects technology, providing filmmakers with more and better tools to visualize their exotic conceptions. But **Star Wars** is not just a bundle of fancy tricks. The exuberance of its story line, the sheer old-fashioned magic of outer space and aliens and good guys vs. bad guys, all of these combine to make the quintessential science fiction image. More than anything, **Star Wars** is a lot of fun to watch.

And surely this is the heart of the SF film, this exuberant sense of delight in the glories of outer space, and man's adventure therein. Science fiction movies of the past tended towards didacticism, preachiness, clumsy satire, overwhelming atomic paranoia. And while science fiction remains an ideal vehicle for social and philosophical messages, very few good films of this type have ever been made. **Star Wars** is undoubtedly a prototype, the first of a series of thoroughly good SF movies that have yet to be made. This is the film that will point the way: hereafter, the only advances can be in characterization and story line.

Our history covers the entire span of the SF film, from Melies's first flickering efforts, to the glorious cinematic images of **Star Wars**. Ours is a selective study, covering only those films we consider particularly significant, either for story line or special effects, or interesting as a movie experience. Sometimes, even bad films are worth viewing (and considering) for specific reasons. "Science fiction" has been narrowly defined here; we have with very few exceptions, strained out horror flicks like **Frankenstein**, and the dozens of monster and exploitation pictures that filled the late '50s. Some must be included as prototypes, but most can fortunately be cast aside without remorse. Also eliminated are television movies, TV series, and fantasy films (the Sinbad series, for example). The selection of films reflects the personal biases and whims of the editors, who take complete responsibility for their choices, and wish they had the space to include more. Since this is a picture book, we have made a real effort to include large, interesting stills from all the major motion pictures mentioned in the book. Sometimes our choices have been constrained by budgetary considerations and the serendipitous availability of the stills themselves, but we think we have managed to provide a representative selection of pictures from all periods in the history of the SF film, including a number of shots never before seen in any other publication of this type. We owe a special word of thanks to Roger Jellinek, Editor-in-Chief at Times Books, for his patience and consideration, and to Ray Bradbury, the well-known American author, for his scintillating introduction. And now, we invite you to join us in celebrating the eightieth birthday of a grand old lady, the SF film, as the golden years of fantastic cinema finally begin. Undeniably, there are many greater things to come!

Douglas Menville, Hollywood, Calif.
R. Reginald, San Bernardino, Calif.
August 10, 1977

MOON VOYAGES AND METAL MAIDENS (1895–1929)

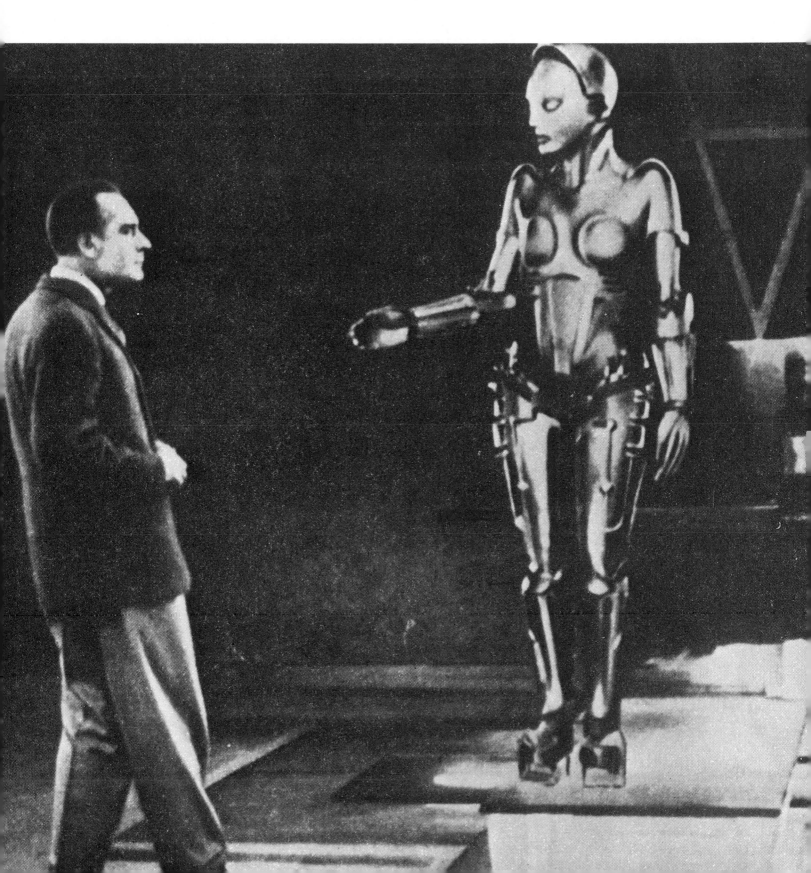

It was no accident that the first professional writer to become involved with the motion picture was a science fiction writer—H. G. Wells. He had been fascinated by the whole concept of moving pictures and had eagerly watched the progress of the new-born medium, from the first experiments in the 1880s, through the development of the Edison Kinetoscope, to the refined projectors that threw images onto a screen. In 1888, Wells had published the first, rough version of what was later to become his first novel. Called at first **The Chronic Argonauts**, it was expanded, after several subsequent drafts, into **The Time Machine**, and published in final, definitive form in 1895.

Although Wells himself was unable to recall the circumstances when asked years later, it seems likely that this novel was suggested by the phenomenon of motion picture film itself. He saw in film the extraordinary potential of visual expression for the far-ranging ideas and concepts swirling around in his mind, a potential which fascinated him throughout most of his life, and which he relentlessly pursued well into the 1930s. In 1929 he wrote: "I believe that if I had my life to live over again I might devote myself entirely to working for the cinema…" And again, in the introduction to his unproduced scenario, **The King Who Was a King**, (1929): "[Motion pictures are] a means of expression exceeding in force, beauty and universality any that have hitherto been available for mankind."

If Wells was fascinated by the cinema, British motion picture pioneer Robert W. Paul was no less fascinated by Wells's **Time Machine**, which he had read in its first magazine serialization in 1894. Having developed a motion picture projector of his own, Paul saw in Wells's remarkable adventure the ideal vehicle for a new and unique system of entertainment, and wasted no time in contacting Wells. Wells was stimulated and delighted by Paul's theatrical concepts, and the result was a joint patent application taken out by the two men in October of 1895, for a kind of multimedia "experience" in which the audience is taken on a simulated voyage into the past and future.

The patent proposed the use of slides, motion pictures, colored lights, currents of air, and even movements of the audience itself to further the illusion. Thus, in one incredible leap forward, Paul and Wells anticipated techniques that were not employed until the 1950s and later, including an approximation of today's "Senssurround" process. (A very similar modern experience was the voyage around the Moon, for years one of the most popular attractions at Disneyland; it utilized film, sound effects, realistic surroundings, and vibrating seats to simulate an actual trip in a rocket.) Further, they anticipated film techniques such as cut-backs, close-ups, fades, dis-

The intrepid aviator peddles over the roofs of Belleville, in the early Zecca film, *La Machine Volante* (*The Flying Machine*), released in France in 1901.

solves, and dolly shots, not to mention the general idea of the photoplay itself, which was not to evolve until many years later. We are accustomed to thinking of Wells as a writer, the forecaster of many of the modern scientific marvels we enjoy today, but with this ancient patent application, he and Paul anticipated an entire art form to come.

Thus, the first important motion picture "experience" should have been a science fiction experience, SF film should have had its birth, and the art of the cinema should have taken a giant step forward at a very early point in cinematic history. Unfortunately, it was not to be. The extraordinary Past-Present-Future Machine was never built because of lack of funds. Paul dropped the project, and never completed the formalities necessary to secure the patent; Wells, greatly stimulated by the concept, went on to produce his finest SF novels in the ensuing decade. **The Island of Dr. Moreau** (1896), **The Invisible Man** (1897), **The War of the Worlds** (1898), **When the Sleeper Wakes** (1899), **The First Men in the Moon** (1901), **The Food of the Gods** (1904), **In the Days of the Comet** (1906), and **The War in the Air** (1908), later provided filmmakers with a wealth of ideas for SF films, both directly and indirectly.

All of these novels were either filmed outright, or had their ideas incorporated into dozens of early pictures; they have continued to surface in version after version throughout the history of the SF film. Wells, and to a lesser degree, Jules Verne, have proved to be the dominant literary influences behind the development of the SF film, with Wells taking an active part during his own lifetime; their works continue to provide story material for new films even today.

If Wells, then, was not the direct progenitor of the SF film, who was? The answer to this question is not a simple one, but in all probability the credit should be given to the French film pioneer, Georges Melies. Film historians in the past have customarily accorded him the honor of having made the first real SF film, **A Trip to the Moon**, in 1902. But quite a number of pictures containing SF elements appeared prior to this date, most of them poking fun at the new marvels of scientific discovery and the Machine Age.

The earliest SF films appeared in 1897, a year after Melies began producing the first of his "magical, mystical and trick films," and were only a few minutes in duration. **The Sausage Machine** (Biograph) turned dogs into strings of sausage; **Making Sausages**, by British filmmaker George A. Smith, "improved" on the recipe by adding cats, ducks, and old boots! The discovery of the X-ray in 1895 was burlesqued by Smith in **The X-Ray Fiend** or **X-Rays**, which had a professor's machine revealing the embracing skeletons of two lovers. Melies produced his own, more ingenious version of this idea in 1898: **Les Rayons Roentgen (A Novice at X-Rays)** showed the subject's skeleton walk right out of his body, which fell to the floor in a heap!

The most significant film of 1897, however, and the one that may be the first true SF film, probably drew its inspiration both from then-current technology and literature: Melies's **Gugusse et l'Automate (Gugusse and the Automaton)**, also known as **The Clown and the Automaton**, is lost to us today, but contemporary accounts indicate that it portrayed the screen's first mechanical person, very possibly female. If so, she was the prototype for one of the mainstays of SF film—the robot—and the direct ancestor of the female automaton in **Metropolis** 29 years later. The word "robot" was unknown at this time, not being coined until 1921 by the Czech writer Karel Capek, in his play, **R. U. R. (Rossum's Universal Robots)**.

So we have a strong case for Melies as the first SF filmmaker; certainly, he provided a seminal influence on this very early period. Melies turned the camera's lens away from reality, and made it tell a story, exploring the fantastic, the humorous, and the bizarre in hundreds of different variations. His concept of "artificially arranged scenes" was to culminate in the sophisticated editing techniques of today's filmmakers. Having developed an impressive bag of cinematic trick effects,

Two stills from Melies's pioneer short, *Un Voyage dans la Lune* (*A Trip to the Moon*), released in France in 1902.

Melies employed them with great success in a never-ending stream of short films, many of them dealing with fantasy and the supernatural; relatively few are classifiable as SF.

His fellow innovators in France, Auguste and Louis Lumiere, preferred, on the whole, to stick with more documentary and realistic subjects, but in 1898 even they succumbed to the antic call, and produced their version of the popular ''sausage machine'' theme. **Charcuterie Mecanique (Mechanical Butcher Shop** or **Mechanical Butcher)** showed a steam-driven machine which produced ham, bacon, spare ribs, sausages, etc., from live pigs. True to the Lumiere ethic, this was a little less fanciful than the earlier versions—at least the proper raw material was used!

By 1899, Melies's fantastic novelties had become so popular that other filmmakers were imitating—and even pirating—his productions. For example, it comes as something of a shock to discover a film called **A Trip to the Moon** in 1899, but this turns out to be merely a pirated retitled version of Melies's 1898 fantasy, **The Astronomer's Dream**. Nevertheless, we are still haunted by

The denizens of the Moon, from Melies's *Un Voyage dans la Lune (A Trip to the Moon)*, released in 1902. Melies's bizarre imagination is clearly evident in the grotesque features of his aliens.

the possiblity of a pre-Melies moon voyage film: on a playbill for the Court Theatre, New Road, Brighton, England, dated "about 1900," is the notice: **"From Earth to Moon: The Latest Fantastic Picture."** Did someone actually beat out Melies, or is this another title for the 1899 pirated film mentioned earlier? No one knows for sure. The estimated date could be' so far off that it might actually be Melies's 1902 film, retitled for British distribution.

The year 1901 ushered in a new century—the beginning of the Age of Electricity, the miracle force which was rapidly being harnessed to do everything from illuminating Thomas Edison's new bulbs, and running his Kinetoscope, to curing disease. Cecil Hopworth's **The Electricity Cure** sparked a long line of "electrical" comedy films, including **The Electrical Goose** (1905), **The Electric Hotel** (1906), **The Electric Belt** (1907), **Liquid Electricity** (1907), **The Electric Servant** (1909), and **The Electric Vitaliser** (1910).

Edison's first contribution to the rapidly growing SF film field was his version of the already overcrowded sausage machine, **Fun in a Butcher Shop** (1901), directed by Edwin S. Porter, who was destined for much greater things. Dogs into sausages again—nothing new here; but in 1904 Edison and Porter turned things around and had sausages turning into dogs, in **The Dog Factory**!

It was a Frenchman named Zecca, however, who produced the most important SF film of 1901 one that opened yet another thematic direction, and vividly pictured one of man's earliest dreams. From Icarus and da Vinci, to Montgolfier's balloons, man has constantly experimented with flight, trying to develop ways to free himself from the restrictions of earth. At the turn of the century, a great dispute raged over whether the heavier-than-air ship (aeronef), or the lighter-than-air dirigible (aerostat), would be the mainstay of future aviation, and many bizarre experiments were being conducted with both kinds of craft. Jules Verne wrote about both: **Five Weeks in a Balloon** (1863) was the first of his incredibly popular "imaginary voyages," and a seminal work in the development of modern science fiction; **Robur the Conqueror** (1886) revealed the power of the amazing, heavier-than-air ship "Albatross."

Prophetically, Zecca opted for the latter type of craft in his film, and two years before the Wright Brothers' historic flight, became the first filmmaker to portray the individual aviator, smiling and waving his hat, as he pedals what resembles a cross between a torpedo and a bicycle over the rooftops of Belleville. The film was called, appropriately enough, **La Machine Volante (The Flying Machine).**

By now, the industrious Melies had over 400 films listed in the **Star Film Catalogue** and they were popular on both sides of the Atlantic. Combining ideas from Verne's **From the Earth to the**

Moon (1865), and Wells's **The First Men in the Moon** (1901), Melies put together his most ambitious and longest film to date in 1902, **Un Voyage Dans la Lune (A Trip to the Moon).** Here was (probably) the first picture to deal with interplanetary flight, a major subject in SF literature since Lucian's work in the second century A.D. Although frivolous and occasionally lapsing into pure fantasy, this film stands as a landmark of SF cinema. Its few flickering minutes present a virtual catalog of images and ideas to come: satire of science and scientists; space travel; an alien landscape with bizarre plant life; the first contact (and inevitable battle) with monstrous extraterrestrials; and an amazingly prophetic splashdown of the returning capsule. Its vivacity, humor, unusual subject matter, and amazing special effects made it an immediate hit, and many of its images are repeated in later SF films.

For example, the giant wheels, cogs, and belching chimneys of the Astronomic Club's foundries (also inspired by Verne) can be seen in **Metropolis** (1926), **Things to Come** (1936), and in the satirical, near-SF comedies, **A Nous la Liberte** (Rene Clair, 1931), and Chaplin's **Modern Times** (1936). The huge space gun was refined and utilized for another moon voyage in **Things to Come**, and Wells's insectoid aliens popped up again in **First Men in The Moon** (1919 and 1964), and **Five Million Years to Earth** (1967).

With the success of Melies's **Trip**, the SF film becomes recognizable as a genre for the first time. Dozens of imitations appeared during the next few years: Segundo de Chomon produced **Viaje a la Luna (A Trip to the Moon)** (1903), **Voyage a la Planete Jupiter (A Trip to Jupiter)** (1907) (in which a king climbs a ladder to Jupiter in a dream, passing each of the planets in turn, and receiving their salutes), and **New Trip to the Moon** (1909). Gaston Velle contributed **Voyage Autour d'une Etoile (Voyage Around a Star)** (1906), in which the method of transportation is a giant soap bubble, and **A Moonlight Dream** (1905) in which a drunk rides a chimney to the Moon. Sigmund Lubin, who had pirated Melies's **Astronomer's Dream** in 1899, now boldly pirated his **Trip to the Moon** as well, releasing it under the misleading title, **A Trip to Mars** (1903).

Although these imitations and rip-offs were of some concern to Melies, he forged ahead with an even grander project, determined to out-imagine his competitors. Spending the enormous sum of $7,500, he produced in 1904 a 24-minute film, **Le Voyage a Travers l'Impossible (The Impossible Voyage).** The story is basically the same as that of **A Trip to the Moon**, only more elaborate: members of the "Institute of Incoherent Geography" discuss the construction of an incredible machine which combines all known devices of locomotion—automobiles, dirigibles, submarines, rockets, etc.—into one long vehicle. Called the "Automabouloff," after its eccentric inventor,

The wreck of the aerial train, from *Le Voyage a Travers l'Impossible* (*The Impossible Voyage*) (Melies, 1904).

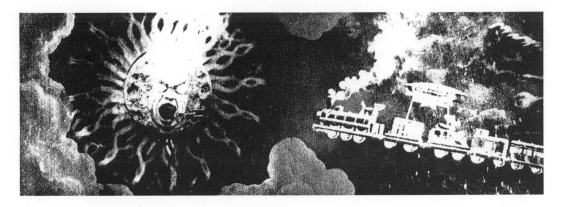

The Automabouloff, from Melies's *Le Voyage a Travers l'Impossible* (*The Impossible Voyage*).

Crazyloff, it is constructed in the heart of familiarly belching foundries, as the learned scientists pore over fantastic maps and charts to plan their voyage around the world.

The 14 intrepid explorers take off in their space train from the summit of a mountain, and soon attain a majestic speed of 300 miles an hour. Hurtling through space, the scientists fly down the throat of the rising sun, barely escaping a solar eruption. Then they visit the aurora borealis, are frozen, and thawed out by an explosion. After a trip to the bottom of the ocean, they finally return to earth to receive honors and decorations for their magnificent voyage. Although a somewhat self-conscious satire of scientific societies, the film is a masterpiece of comic invention and technological achievement; in it, Melies brought to fruition all his abilities as showman, storyteller, artist, caricaturist, and camera wizard.

Meanwhile, in England, Robert W. Paul, apparently undaunted by his abortive Time Machine project, was now producing films of his own. The influence of Melies's **Impossible Voyage** is clearly apparent in Paul's 1905 film, **The ? Motorist**. Directed by Walter Booth, Paul's version is more restrained and quietly amusing than the earlier picture. A young couple in a motor car demonstrate the perils of speeding as, chased by a policeman, they fly off into space, motor across the clouds, pay a call to the sun, and finally end up calmly driving around the rings of Saturn. But retribution awaits below: the car rides off the rings and gracefully descends to earth, crashing through the roof of a Court of Justice. The errant couple manage to disguise themselves and escape the law.

Paul's film offers a questionable moral, perhaps, but it was understandably popular with the public. This early example of the "policeman-as-buffoon" syndrome was to reach its apex in the Keystone Kops films of Mack Sennett, from 1912 through 1920, and is still good for a laugh today.

Paul's director, Walter Booth, was a cartoonist and magician like Melies, but unlike the innovative Frenchman, Booth's reputation has been unjustly neglected over the years. One of the unsung pioneers of the SF film, Booth directed an interesting series of pictures dealing with futuristic aircraft, such as **The Aerocab and Vacuum Provider** (1909), **The Aerial Submarine** (1910), and **The Aerial Anarchists** (1911). Booth's most significant creation, however, was **The Airship Destroyer** (1909), produced by Charles Urban. Once again H. G. Wells was the inspiration: his novel, **The War in the Air**, had been published just a year previously, prophesying with terrible accuracy the perils of aerial bombardment. Wells's novel was not the first work to portray warfare in the heavens (E. Douglas Fawcett's **Hartmann the Anarchist** (1893), George Griffith's **The Angel of the Revolution** (1894), and Verne's **Master of the World** (1904) were earlier), but his remains the best known, and its influence is plain on Booth's film.

Driving through the clouds, in Robert Paul's *The ? Motorist*, released in Britain in 1905.

A young inventor of a radio-controlled aerial torpedo uses his invention to repel a dirigible bombardment of London. The models and special effects, as bomb explosions destroy London's buildings and railroads, are particularly well done, and amazingly realistic; and the young man's rescue of his girl friend manages to inject the traditional love interest in an unobtrusive manner, something later SF films would have done well to emulate.

Also known as **Aerial Warfare, Aerial Torpedo**, and by several other more cumbersome titles, Booth's picture was released in the U. S. in 1910 as **The Battle in the Clouds**. Looking at this film today, we can see immediately that its greatest importance lies not in its prophecy of aerial warfare and ground-to-air missiles, but in the fact that it was the first SF film to take its subject seriously. Heretofore, most of the films produced could be considered SF only by stretching the definition, with elements of fantasy and dream often outweighing the "science." Then, too, the approach was invariably a comedic one, poking fun at science and scientists and their crazy machines. Now, science is taken in deadly earnest on the screen for the first time; the SF film had taken its first steps towards eventual maturity.

The success of Booth's film led to many imitations, as always, but Booth himself took the idea one step further in his own picture, **The Aerial Anarchists** (1911). Apparently directly suggested by E. Douglas Fawcett's novel, **Hartmann the Anarchist**, this 15-minute drama showed the construction of a gigantic airship by a group of anarchists, who use it to devastate London by aerial bombardment. Bridges, fortresses, and St. Paul's Cathedral all fall to the terrorists' attack.

But Walter Booth was not the first filmmaker to portray futuristic aircraft: in 1908, J. Stuart Blackton had produced and directed for Vitagraph one of the earliest American SF films, taking Zecca's 1901 flying machine a step forward from fantasy into the distant future. **The Airship; or, One Hundred Years Hence** sent the SF film towards one of its most exciting and provocative directions. Blackton's vision of the 21st century includes streamlined aircraft, passenger-carrying dirigibles, and a refinement of Zecca's aerialist into the ever-present policeman, pursuing speeders on an aerocycle. While not very original, and still in the comic vein, this film was nevertheless genuine SF, and demonstrated the unrivalled potential of the cinema for visualizing the future.

The future has always fascinated mankind—we all enjoy peering into tomorrow, to see visualizations of futuristic aircraft, automobiles, cities, machinery, and people. Forecasting the future is one of the things that written SF has done so successfully. In film, however, visions have too often been disappointing—not enough detail, too much glitter without substance, nightmarish pictures of a tomorrow we'd rather not see. But the potential is there, and when realized, as in **Metropolis** (1926), **Things to Come** (1936), **2001** (1968), and **Star Wars** (1977), there is nothing more impressive.

That this potential was immediately recognized by filmmakers is evident in the flood of futuristic films that followed **The Airship**. **Life in the Next Century** (Lux, 1909) portrayed people travelling in electrically-powered chairs. **Looking Forward** (Thanhouser, 1910) borrowed the Wellsian concept of suspended animation from **When the Sleeper Wakes** (1899) to show a young scientist awaking after a hundred years in a world ruled by women. This film initiated a number of sexist imitations in which female-dominated future societies were portrayed, burlesquing the then-current suffragette movement. **One Hundred Years After** (Pathe, 1911), **In the Year 2000** (Solax, 1912), **In the Year 2014** (Universal, 1914), and **Percy Pumpernickel, Soubrette** (Kalem, 1914) were almost identical treatments of the same idea.

All of these visions were, like the majority of SF films before them, comic ones. But the cinema was also beginning to deal with grimmer and more serious futures. Aerial outlaws bombard a bullion ship and kidnap the heroine in **The Pirates of 1920** (Cricks and Martin, 1911), while **Aerial Anarchists** destroy London in the film of the same name. But terrorists were only a minor threat in the early 1900s.

The fear of foreign invasion had been gathering force in the public mind ever since the 1870s, fed by a deluge of hawkish literature such as George Chesney's **The Battle of Dorking** (1871), which spurred that fear to white heat. Published as a realistic narrative of the invasion of England by German forces in the near future, it sent shock waves of alarm throughout the world. Although

The young fisherman, from *Deux Cent Mille Lieues sous les Mers; ou, Le Cauchemar d'un Pecheur (20,000 Leagues Under the Seas; or, A Fisherman's Nightmare)*, a 1907 Melies production.

other accounts of imaginary invasions had been published before, none had the narrative vigor and immediate impact of **Dorking**, which created an entire sub-genre of SF, known as the "future war" novel. Hundreds of books and pamphlets appeared in the years following, with warning after warning of imminent invasions by Germany, Russia, and the hordes of Asia. This last threat was the subject of several novels by the British SF writer M. P. Shiel, including **The Yellow Danger** (1898), **The Yellow Wave** (1905), and **The Dragon** (1913) (later retitled **The Yellow Peril**). These novels, together with Sax Rohmer's popular Fu Manchu series, which began in 1913, sent British and American xenophobia soaring to new heights.

Then, in 1914, war in Europe became a reality—the Hun was no longer an idle threat. Americans feared involvement, and eventual invasion became a real possibility. And with the Germans already fighting, could the Yellow Peril be far behind?

This mass paranoia was picked up and mirrored in the rapidly-growing SF film. **The Scenario Writer's Dream** (Universal, 1915) depicts the invasion and destruction of New York City by aircraft equipped with death rays. In **A Zeppelin Attack on New York** (1917) the Kaiser's zeppelin fleet wipes out the city. **The Battle Cry of Peace** (Vitagraph, 1915) and **The Fall of a Nation** (Vitagraph, 1916) portray the invasion of the United States by Germanic troops. The latter was filmed as a spectacle, employing some 20,000 extras, and was based on the little-known novel by Thomas A. Dixon, whose earlier book, **The Clansman**, was filmed by D. W. Griffith as **The Birth of a Nation** (1915). **The Fall of a Nation**, which boasted a musical score by Victor Herbert, depicted vividly the horrors of an occupied America, finally victorious through an underground revolution led by women soldiers.

Griffith, who has been called "one of the three authentic geniuses produced by the cinema," had previously written and directed two prehistoric pictures, **Man's Genesis** (Biograph, 1912) and **Brute Force** (Biograph, 1913), both of which featured cave men and dinosaurs, and may have been inspired by the 1907 publication of Jack London's novel, **Before Adam**. As crude as they

The underwater kingdom, from Melies's *20,000 Leagues Under the Seas* (1907).

were, they served as a training ground for Griffith's later film triumphs, and provided patterns for the later development of the prehistoric drama, as typified by **One Million B. C.** (UA, 1940), and **When the Dinosaurs Ruled the Earth** (Hammer, 1970).

In 1916, Griffith added his contribution to the foreign invasion films. **The Flying Torpedo** (Triangle) was produced by Griffith from a scenario by Robert M. Baker and John Emerson, who also starred as the male lead. It was merely a more elaborate remake of Urban's 1909 **The Airship Destroyer**, but with some impressive special effects by the McCarthy brothers, who were later to make a name for themselves in this same area. An eccentric detective-story writer invents a radio-controlled aerial torpedo, with which he foils an invasion of Southern California by an airborne Asiatic horde.

The feature film was now a reality, with audiences accustomed to sitting through pictures several hours in length; the star system was also gathering impetus. The SF film was being used

The giant octopus, from the 1916 silent version of *20,000 Leagues Under the Sea* (Universal).

primarily as a forum for social commentary and propaganda, instead of mere brainless entertainment. In France, this meant that the age of Melies was over.

In 1907, he had opened two new directions for the SF film. **Deux Cent Mille Lieues Sous les Mers; ou, Le Cauchemar d'un Pecheur (20,000 Leagues Under the Seas; or, A Fisherman's Nightmare)** was the first. Melies borrowed the title from Verne, but very little else, in this elaborate, hand-colored fantasy extravaganza.

A young fisherman dreams of taking a submarine trip to the ocean's floor, where he meets crabs, monstrous fish, and other marine monsters closely patterned after those illustrated in the Verne novel. But he also encounters more pleasant denizens: mermaids, a ballet of beautiful naiads, and the Queen of the Starfish.

Also known as **Under the Seas**, the film was actually a burlesque of Verne, and contrasted amusingly with the writer's sober and moralistic approach. The first serious adaption of **20,000**

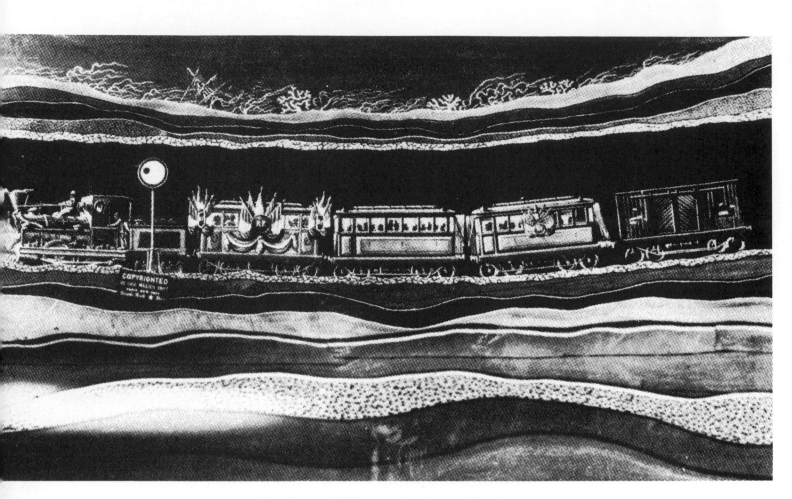

Trains travelling beneath the English Channel, in Melies's 1907 classic, *Le Tunnel sous la Manche; ou, Le Cauchemar Franco-Anglais* (*The Tunnel Under the English Channel*).

Leagues Under the Sea did not appear until 1916 (Universal), for which the Williamson brothers provided some fascinating underwater special effects, including a large dummy octopus with coiled spring and india-rubber arms. This was probably the first film to utilize underwater photography, and also helped focus public attention on the German U-boat menace at this stage of World War I. Portions of Verne's **Mysterious Island** were also incorporated into the screenplay, as well as a sequence revealing Captain Nemo's origin as Count Dakkar of India.

The second Melies film of 1907, also a dream adventure, was **Le Tunnel Sous la Manche; ou, Le Cauchemar Franco-Anglais (The Tunnel Under the English Channel; or, the Franco-English Nightmare)**. Also known as **Tunnelling the English Channel,** the film describes the simultaneous dream of King Edward VII of England and President Fallieres of France about building a Channel Tunnel. Electric drilling machines and scores of men work feverishly to complete the link between Dover and Calais. Finally, the first trains pass through the tunnel, and there are great celebrations on both sides. But then a catastrophic collision awakens both dreamers, and alarmed by the premonition, the rulers decide to postpone the project.

These and other films could not save Melies's career—his popularity had finally begun to wane, both in France and in America. Audiences were becoming more sophisticated; the feature-length film was beginning to develop; new filmmakers, with new and more serious ideas and techniques, were grabbing a large share of the market.

Promotional drawing for Melies's last SF film, *A la Conquete du Pole* (*The Conquest of the Pole*), released in France in 1912.

Melies's fortunes plummeted, until in 1912, his last year of production, he made only four films. One of these was a final attempt at the kind of spectacular ''imaginary voyage'' that had proved so popular years before, **A la Conquete du Pole (The Conquest of the Pole)**. Choosing two areas of popular interest, aviation and the Arctic (which was still largely unexplored), Melies told the wacky tale of Professor Maboul, who invents a bulky aircraft called the Aerobus. In it, he and a group of explorers visit the North Pole, where they encounter the screen's first real monster, a gigantic, pipe-smoking snow giant that devours several of the members of the expedition. This prototypical ''abominable snowman'' is defeated by cannon fire, and sinks back beneath the ice after regurgitating the unfortunate explorers. The men subsequently find themselves attracted by, and stuck to, the North Pole. This idea was Melies's farewell tribute to his mentor, Jules Verne—it had appeared in **Le Sphinx des Glaces (The Sphinx of the Ice-Fields)**, published in 1897.

Thus, even in his decline, Melies pioneered one more direction in which SF film was to go: beginning with **The Lost World** in 1926, and **King Kong** in 1933, giant monsters were to provide the basis for dozens of SF film in the 1950s and thereafter.

The Conquest of the Pole was one of Melies's best efforts, amusingly and ingeniously produced. But it could not save his career. During World War I, and the two decades which followed, Melies, now an anachronism, was barely able to eke out an existence. Finally, after a long illness, the ''father of the science fiction film'' died in 1938, his grim decline in pitiful contrast to the light-hearted, rollicking fantasy films he had given the world.

13

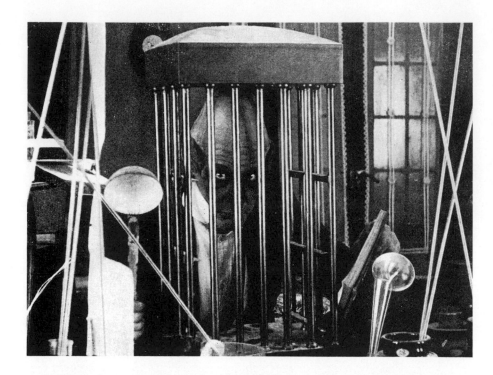

The mad scientist, from Abel Gance's strange experimental picture, *La Folie du Docteur Tube* (*The Madness of Dr. Tube*), released in France in 1914.

A popular play by Richard Ganthony, **A Message from Mars** (1899) was filmed as a silent short in 1909, and again in 1913 in Britain, introducing yet another popular subject for SF films—aliens from outer space. The 1913 feature version starred E. Holman Clark as a cloaked, outcast Martian sent to earth by the God of Mars to cure a single mortal (Charles Hawtrey) of selfishness; having accomplished this worthy act, Clarke can be reinstated on Mars. In future SF films, the benign visitor from space was to be far outnumbered by the alien invader bent on destruction and conquest, the direct legacy of Wells's **The War of the Worlds**, published in 1898. But nevertheless, **A Message from Mars** deserves note as the earliest treatment of this subject on film, albeit one owing more to metaphysics than to science.

In 1914, Abel Gance, who was to take up the mantle of the SF film in France, experimenting with bizarre visual techniques, and avant-garde subject matter, directed **La Folie du Docteur Tube (The Madness of Dr. Tube)**, a short experimental film dealing with a mad doctor who succeeds in breaking up light waves with a mechanism of crystal tubes. Gance's ingenious use of distorting lenses, mirrors, out-of-focus photography, and other camera tricks created some striking visuals, but the obscure symbolism of its rather thin content kept the film from release for several years. Gance—as always—was way ahead of the world cinema audience; he created a cinematic world of distortion and deformity years before the German picture, **The Cabinet of Dr. Caligari** (1919), was to set the pattern for the horror film in both Europe and America. It is Dr. Tube, therefore, who can claim the honor of being the screen's first real mad scientist, a staple of both SF and horror films for years to come.

Nineteen fourteen, besides marking the advent of the "Great War" that had been predicted so often in SF books and films, also saw the release by Pathe of the first serial with elements of SF, **The Exploits of Elaine**, a 14-chapter thriller. It starred Pearl White, who had become America's endangered sweetheart in an earlier serial, **The Perils of Pauline**; here, she tries to bring to justice her father's murderer, a sinister hooded villain known as "The Clutching Hand." It also brought to the screen the popular Craig Kennedy, scientific detective (played by Creighton Hale), who was to appear in a number of future serials. His creator, Arthur B. Reeve, also co-authored the story and screenplay for **Elaine**, and produced a novelization of it for Harper's.

As Elaine makes her perilous way through chapters with such titles as "The Twilight Sleep," "The Poisoned Room," "The Vampire," "The Death Ray," "The Life Current," and "The Devil Worshippers," she encounters such pseudo-scientific paraphernalia as deadly gases, an infra-red death ray, and an electrical apparatus that brings her back from the dead!

So popular was this combination of science and super-villain that it made well over a million dollars for Pathe, and set the pattern for many serials to come, well into the 1950s. More immediately, it spawned two sequels, **The New Exploits of Elaine** (1915, 10 chapters), and **The Romance of Elaine** (1915, 12 chapters).

The inevitable imitations followed: **The Black Box** (1915) was Universal's entry into the SF

"The 'Clutching Hand' did this! I shall consecrate my life to bring this man to justice."—*The Exploits of E-laine* (1914).

serial arena, novelized by the popular writer of international intrigues, E. Phillips Oppenheim. This time the scientific detective was "Sanford Quest, criminologist" (Herbert Rawlinson), and the SF elements included a televiewer that could be hooked up to any telephone, an electronic thought transference machine, electrically-assisted hypnotism, an invisibility cloak—and an ape man!

The Diamond from the Sky (American Film Manufacturing Co., 1915) was an attempt to outdo all previous serials, in length, if nothing else—it was 30 chapters (60 reels) long, and had tinted sequences. Written by a newspaperman named Roy L. McCardell, it was the only professional entry in a newspaper scenario contest offering a $10,000 prize. McCardell won over 19,002 other entries and later published a novelization of the vast serial, which was directed by William Desmond Taylor, and starred Mary Pickford's sister Lottie, when Mary refused the role.

The story is only borderline SF, revolving around a huge diamond, the core of a meteor that falls to the earth in Colonial Virginia in 1615. It saves a young English adventurer, Sir Arthur Stanley, from certain death at the hands of Indians, and is passed down in his family from generation to generation as a "charm against harm."

The fortunes of this enormous gem were so enthralling to audiences that a sequel was pro-

(above)   *Fantomas* (Louis Feuillade, 1913/1914).

(below)   *Les Vampires*, another serial by Louis Feuillade, featured this comely lass (1915).

(above right)   *The Diamond from the Sky* (American Film Manufacturing Company, 1915) featured a huge diamond meteorite. Here Vivian gives Arthur an injection while Esther looks on.

(right)   *Fantomas*, from the serial of the same name (Louis Feuillade, 1913/1914).

(above)   Quest and Lenora receive the message from Laura, in *The Black Box* (Universal, 1915).

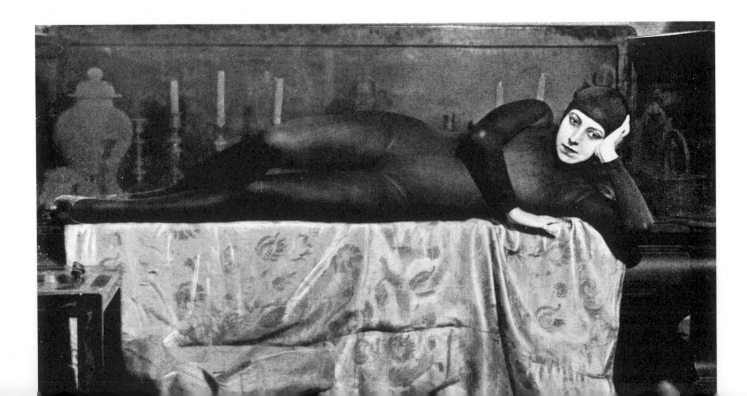

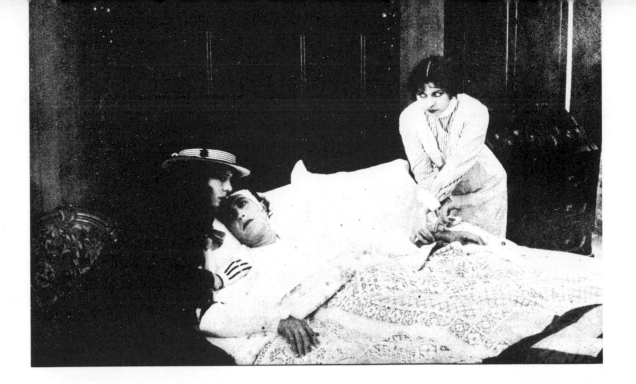

duced the following year, written by film historian Terry Ramsaye, and cleverly entitled **Sequel to the Diamond from the Sky** (Mutual). It was first released as a feature film, then as a four-part serial; it chronicled the theft and eventual recovery of the charmed diamond.

Traces of SF appeared in the stylish French serials of Louis Feuillade, **Fantomas** (1913-14), **Les Vampires** (1915), and **Judex** (1916-17), but in Germany, the SF serial took a more ominous turn. Inspired by Mary Shelley's horror classic **Frankenstein**, published in 1818, Otto Rippert directed a six-part serial in 1916 called **Homunkulus der Fuhrer (Homunculus the Leader)**, based on a novel by Robert Reinert. Homunculus (played by Danish actor Olaf Fonss) is an artificial human, created by Professor Hansen and his assistant Rodin; the similarities and contrasts between this Germanic android and Mary Shelley's monster are striking.

Like the monster, Homunculus is created in a laboratory, but chemically, in a retort, and not from parts of dead bodies. Where the Frankenstein monster is a horrible, grotesque travesty of a human being, Homunculus is strikingly handsome, and develops into a man of iron will and impressive intellect. But he and the Frankenstein monster both develop feelings of rejection when the secrets of their birth are revealed to them—they become outcasts and wanderers in far countries, searching for love and understanding, but encountering only fear and loathing wherever they go. Homunculus is called "the man without a soul, the devil's servant," until he finally comes to despise all mankind, and determines to use his super-human powers to take revenge. Whereas the Frankenstein monster wishes revenge only on his creator, Homunculus makes himself dictator of a large country, and proceeds to oppress the entire population in terrifying ways. He disguises himself as a worker, inciting riots which he then crushes ruthlessly.

Finally, he sets off a world war. At this, the gods themselves feel that Homunculus is too evil to live and, since man cannot stop him, they send a thunderbolt from the heavens to strike him down. The same lightning that gave life to Frankenstein's monster (in the definitive 1931 screen version) has destroyed Professor Hansen's "man without a soul." Although an unsatisfactorily supernatural ending, death by lightning and similar means has persisted as one of the stocks in trade of the SF and horror film.

The unsettling elements utilized in this serial—sado-masochistic behavior, implied impotence and homosexuality, and a lust for power and destruction—became common in the German films of this period, and during the 1920s and '30s. But most unsettling of all is the clear foreshadowing of Hitler and his cult of Aryan supremacy. This time the prophetic powers of the SF film were grim indeed!

Homunkulus has largely been overlooked as an influence on German cinema in favor of **The Cabinet of Dr. Caligari** (Decla-Bioscop, 1919), but its attitudes and images are plainly reflected in the later work of Fritz Lang and other German directors. **Caligari** merely accelerated the patterns that **Homunkulus** originated.

Other serials and feature films of this period continued to reflect the fears and uncertainties of their audiences, as the war in Europe dragged on. **Pawns of Mars** (Broadway Star Feature, 1915) was removed in time to the far future, but the message was clear: two great city-states called "Cosmotania" and "Mapadonia" are at war, using futuristic aircraft and wireless rays which explode bombs at a distance. The "Mars" in the title refers not to the planet, but to the God of War.

Abel Glance was still experimenting with SF in France, making **Les Gaz Mortels (The Deadly Gases)** (1916), which contained more truth than science fiction, as many an unfortunate Allied soldier could testify.

Wanting to "do his bit" for the war effort in his overbearing, hawkish manner, William

Homunculus surveys his forces, from *Homunkulus der Fuhrer* (*Homunculus the Leader*), a takeoff on the Frankenstein theme (Otto Rippert, 1916).

Randolph Hearst commissioned Louis Joseph Vance to write a newspaper serial called **Patria**, which was subsequently turned into a 15-part serial in 1916-17. It was one of the more spectacular SF efforts of the day, starring Irene Castle, Milton Sills, and Warner Oland, who played "Baron Huroki," dictator of America. (Oland was warming up for a later role as the ultimate "Yellow Peril," Dr. Fu Manchu.) In this film, the U. S. is attacked and defeated by an army of allied Japanese and Mexican troops, and the horrors of conquest under an Oriental heel are vividly depicted.

"Doing his bit" meant, to Hearst, that the U. S. should immediately become involved in war against Mexico, Japan, and anybody else we could take on. Why should the Europeans have all the fun? Hearst pulled no punches—no longer were the invaders only vaguely identified as "Asiatics." They were named outright; in fact, the film was so inflammatory that President Woodrow Wilson stepped in and made Pathe cut out many scenes. Even so, it remains an appalling bit of pro-war propaganda, while still being a vivid and exciting SF film. The spectacular climax depicted Irene Castle leading a force of giant super-tanks into battle against hordes of Japanese with flame-throwers invading from Mexico.

A similar serial was **The Yellow Menace** (Serial Film Co., 1916), in which Edwin Stevens, a noted stage actor, played the Oriental conqueror of America, "Ali Singh," a characterization much closer to Fu Manchu in concept than Oland's. Many techniques typical of Sax Rohmer's Devil Doctor are employed throughout the film, including poisonous spiders trained and directed to kill, a video crystal ball used as a spy device, a secret formula for an explosive, and a blinding ray.

From national catastrophe to world catastrophe was but a small step for the SF film. In 1910, Halley's Comet made a spectacular sweep through the heavens, bringing apocalyptic predictions from many quarters. Comets have been thought of as harbingers of disaster throughout history, and SF filmmakers did nothing to dispel these feelings.

The Comet (Kalem, 1910) exploded automobiles, burned houses, and sent the world's population underground in search of water. The last scene depicts a panoramic view of a world in ruins.

Sixteen years before, one of the earliest novels to deal with world destruction, **La Fin du Monde (The End of the World)**, by the French astronomer Camille Flammarion, had been published in the U. S. as **Omega: The Last Days of the World. The Comet** showed the direct influence of this apocalyptic vision, in which a giant comet destroys the earth in the 25th century. Man survives the devastation, however, and raises his civilization to new heights, abolishing war, creating marvels of super-scientific technology, and establishing psychic communication with Mars and

A playbill from *La Fin du Monde* (*The End of the World*) (L'Ecran d'Art, 1930).

Venus. But slowly, water is absorbed into the earth's interior and the world grows progressively colder and drier until, ten million years later, the last man and woman die in each other's arms.

The direct literary progenitor of Olaf Stapledon's **Last and First Men** (1930), this vast work inspired still other catastrophe films: a Danish production, **Verldens Undergang** (Nordisk, 1916), was released in this country as **The End of the World**, starring Emma Thomsen and a spectacular array of special effects. A colliding comet causes fiery devastation, electrical storms, earthquakes, and floods, as millions flee for their lives.

Years later, the indefatigable Abel Gance wrote and directed his version of the Flammarion novel, **La Fin du Monde** (L'Ecran d'Art, 1930), starring himself and a cast of thousands. The book seemed a perfect vehicle for one of his symbolic, idealogical epics, and contains some impressive scenes, although the critics continually chided him for his "inability to be simple." The film was released in a shortened version with English subtitles in 1934.

The Comet's Come-Back (Mutual, 1916) owed more to H. G. Wells's 1906 novel, **In the Days of the Comet,** than to Flammarion. This time, however, the results were not quite so drastic: the comet emits a gas that slows everybody down.

These early films pointed towards still another direction for the SF film, depicting vividly the consequences of nature gone berserk, and the fragility of man's hold on this planet. The SF film was rapidly becoming the ultimate disaster film, destined to be filled with future wars, invasions from other nations and other worlds, devastation of entire cities by giant monsters, and world-wide catastrophes. The early burlesques of scientists and their inventions gone humorously beserk were no longer in vogue; now a more serious note was sounded, against the misuse of technology at the expense of human values, and the inability of man's scientific advances to cope with disasters of a cosmic nature.

Throughout its long career, SF cinema has been the cinema of paranoia, catering to our deepest fears and anxieties. There have been light-hearted exceptions, but very few. Even such films as **Forbidden Planet** (MGM, 1956), and **Star Wars** (Fox, 1977), have their dark sides, their terrifying "id beasts" and "Death Stars." The imagination that has controlled the SF film has been what Susan Sontag astutely calls "the imagination of disaster." It is the excitement of destruction, more than anything else, the savage wonder of battles in space, on distant worlds, and in dim futures, that calls to us and brings us back to the SF film again and again. We can experience the most terrifying destruction, see our deepest fears visualized, and then go out again into the real world where everything is still the same.

The Master Mystery (Octagon, 1918) featured a fake mechanical man, here shown menacing mankind.

This is not a bad thing. Without fantasy, without dreams—even nightmares—we would quickly go insane. SF filmmakers have always provided these dreams for us, violent and cathartic, and their messages and warnings, when not presented in too imbecile a fashion, are worth pondering. Without science fiction movies, as foolish as they often are, our lives would be much the poorer.

Not all SF films of the Teens were heavy-handed, however. The unjustly-overlooked German filmmaker, Harry Piel, directed the first real SF spectacle, **Die Grosse Wette (The Great Bet)**, in 1916. Starring Mizzi Wirth, Ludwig Hartmann, and Piel himself, the film depicts the world of 2000 A. D. in astonishing and imaginative detail, ten years before Fritz Lang's much more famous **Metropolis**. Piel envisions such wonders as an airline cab service, a 21st-century millionaire's palace with all the modern conveniences, robots, and a library whose books can be retrieved by merely pressing a button.

An American millionaire bets his fortune that he can live three days with an automaton, but discovers that the robot has some amusing and frustrating tricks up its mechanical sleeves.

This film was well received in general, and pointed in both directions: backwards to such futuristic comedies as **The Airship; or, One Hundred Years Hence** (1908), and **In the Year 2000** (1912), and forwards to the more serious predictions of **Metropolis** (1926), **High Treason** (1929), **Things to Come** (1936), **2001** (1968), and **Logan's Run** (1976). Only a few films to come, such as **Just Imagine** (1930), and **Sleeper** (1973), were to retain a comic view of the future.

In Denmark, the success of Nordisk with **The End of the World** prompted them to revive cinematic space travel in a more serious fashion than Melies and his peers had treated it. Having destroyed the world, they now proceeded to save it. **Himmelskibet (The Sky Ship** or **Heaven Ship)** (1917), written by Danish film promoter Ole Oleson, and directed by Forest Holger-Madsen, was the first feature-length film to deal with interplanetary flight.

Frederick Jacobsen heads an idealistic expedition to the planet Mars, in a stubby-winged, propellor-driven spaceship named "Excelsior," which looks like an early design for Lindbergh's "Spirit of St. Louis." Mars is a flowery paradise, inhabited by noble, white-robed men and women, garlanded with blossoms and palm (?) fronds in honor of peace. War has been outlawed here, and Jacobsen's inherently violent tendencies (he shoots a bird for lunch) cause him to be hustled away by the Martians to the "Temple of Contemplation," where he must cure himself by self-examination. Purged of evil, he marries the prettiest of the Martian maidens and takes her back to Copenhagen with him so she can persuade the governments to stop World War I.

It was all pretty silly, but maybe it worked: the war ended in 1918, and the film's plea for international peace was somewhat more uplifting than what most SF films had to offer. But as all too often happens, the message outweighed the production and story values.

If peace had come to the world, the robots didn't know it. After years of good-natured spoofing of mechanical servants gone awry, as in **Mechanical Mary Anne** (Hepworth, 1910), **The Mechanical Husband** (LCC, 1910), and **The Mechanical Man** (Universal, 1915), the automaton was suddenly depicted as an object of terror.

A robot which kills from a distance with electrical rays, becoming a criminal mastermind, and spreading fear and death throughout the populace, is featured in **The Master Mystery** (Octagon, 1918), a fifteen-chapter serial. The automaton is later brought down by Houdini, making his unfortunate film debut as the hero. Although "Q the Automaton" turns out to be a fake, with a mad scientist inside, the image was set—from now on, the robot was to appear in countless numbers of SF films as an object of menace, particularly in the serials of the 1930s and '40s. Appearances of his more peaceful brethren, such as Robby the Robot in **Forbidden Planet** (MGM,

1956), and the delightful Laurel and Hardy "'droids" of **Star Wars** (Twentieth Century-Fox, 1977), have been few.

Nineteen nineteen brought the German entry in the "end-of-the-world sweepstakes," **The Arc**, a two-part film based on a novel by Werner Scheff. By this time, the future destruction of civilization was old hat, and the film is more important for the fact that both its director, Richard Oswald, and its cinematographer, Karl Freund (who also shot **Metropolis** for Fritz Lang), later came to the U. S., where they made American films during the 1930s and '40s.

The same year saw the production of a far more important German film, **The Cabinet of Dr. Caligari** (Decla-Bioscop, 1919). Although not a SF film, but dealing with the brilliantly visualized delusions of a madman, this picture helped transform the design of all German films to come, and almost single-handedly created the genre of the horror film. Its striking expressionistic sets influenced art directors on both sides of the Atlantic, and can be seen echoed in both horror and SF films of the 1920s and '30s. Werner Krauss's sinister Dr. Caligari is the prototype of every mad scientist who ever stalked the celluloid, and his somnambulistic servant, Cesare (Conrad Veidt), is the forerunner of every monster who ever kidnapped a heroine.

Finally, 1919 marked the year that brought H. G. Wells to the screen at last. His enthusiasm for the cinema was undimmed by his aborted 1895 project with Robert W. Paul; indeed, Wells had signed a contract for the filming of his novels in 1914, but World War I intervened, and the contract could not be fulfilled. The man who had supplied so many SF film ideas to others had to wait until 1919 to see one of his own works visualized.

A still from the German film *Algol* (1920), displaying the designs of Walther Reimann and Paul Sheerbart. This film has unfortunately been lost.

Unfortunately, **The First Men in the Moon** (Gaumont) was a great disappointment. The adaption was unimaginative, the sets ludicrous, and the injection of the obligatory love interest did nothing to help. J. V. Leigh's direction was uninspired, and the Selenites looked like humanoid potatoes with ping-pong balls for eyes. Even worse, the Grand Lunar resembled a huge-headed "giant baby." Melies's lunar landscapes and lively Selenites back in 1902 were far superior.

The screenplay tampered with Wells's story without improving it: Professor Samson Cavor (Hector Abbas) invents an anti-gravity substance called "Cavorite," which powers a metal sphere that takes him and Rupert Bedford (Lionel d'Aragon) to the moon. After witnessing a lunar sunrise, the two men are captured by Selenites, and taken down into their subterranean civil-

The end of the world, as depicted in *La Mort du Soleil* (*The Death of the Sun*) (Dulac, 1920).

ization. Bedford manages to escape after stunning Cavor and stealing what he incorrectly thinks is the formula for Cavorite. He returns to earth and tries to win the love of Susan (Heather Thatcher), Cavor's niece, telling her that it was the scientist's dying wish that they marry. But Hannibal Hogben (Bruce Gordon), Cavor's wireless operator, is Susan's real love, and when he receives a wireless message from Cavor on the moon, the jig is up for Bedford, and the lovers are united in bliss.

Poor Wells! After all this waiting, he was not to see another SF novel reach the screen until 1932, when the excellent **Island of Lost Souls** would finally do him justice.

The "Roaring Twenties" ushered in another end-of-the-world epic, this time from France. Germaine Dulac's **La Mort du Soleil (The Death of the Sun)** (1920) belongs to the same type of experimental filmmaking as the works of Abel Gance and Marcel L'Herbier, emphasizing visual imagery of a complex artistic nature and extravagant story material. As in all the doomsday films of this period, the usual orgies and mass hysteria prevail.

Only a few tantalizing stills remain from what must have been an extraordinary German SF film of 1920, **Algol**. With extravagant and "decadent" art design by Walther Reimann and poet-architect Paul Sheerbart, and under the direction of Hans Werkmeister, this lost film starred the superb Emil Jannings. An evil interstellar visitor from the Demon Star, Algol, comes to earth to tempt Jannings with a machine that can make him master of the world. Such absolute power corrupts, as always, and Jannings is unable to control the side effects, which include the death of his wife, the ruin of his son, and the abduction of his daughter. At last Jannings comes to his senses and destroys the terrible machine, but is instantly killed. This film was clearly speaking to the German psyche, but its message went unheeded.

A Message from Mars was remade by Metro in 1921, this time starring Bert Lytell, with Alphonz Ethier as the Martian. Like its 1913 predecessor, this story of a selfish young man who is shown the poverty and suffering of humanity by a Martian messenger is more fantasy than SF. Hollywood even took one step further away from reality by making it all a dream!

During the '20s, most Hollywood producers held SF in very low esteem; as a result, no films of any consequence appeared in the U. S. until 1929, with the single exception of **The Lost World** (1925), and even that film was set solidly on earth. Science-fictional gadgets were appropriate as props for serials—robots and death rays continued to proliferate—but invaders from another planet were apparently too far out!

A case in point is a 1921 Pathe serial originally entitled **The Man Who Stole the Moon**, written by veteran serialist Frank Leon Smith, and directed by George B. Seitz (Seitz also starred in the serial, along with June Caprice and Spencer Bennett, and went on to direct the "Andy Hardy" comedies of the 1930s). As originally envisioned by Smith, the story concerned a man and woman who come to Earth from Mars in a spaceship equipped with death rays, determined to conquer the world. The producers, however, thought all this was too fantastic, and converted the Martian villain into an earthly hero complete with his advanced aircraft; they also explained away his powers of teleportation as a magician's illusion, and converted the scenes on Mars with huge super-scientific sets into "an underground citadel in the mountains of Tibet." To top it off, they changed the title to **The Sky Ranger**. No wonder Seitz turned to Andy Hardy!

Fortunately, the European directors were still experimenting with SF. Pierre Benoit's popular 1919 French novel of adventure in the lost kingdom of Atlantis (curiously located under the Sahara Desert), **L'Atlantide**, formed the basis for an expensive production of the same name directed by a Belgian ex-actor named Jacques Feyder. He took a camera crew to Morocco, and cast Stacia Napierkowska, the Comedie Francaise star, as the cruel Queen Antinea, who seduces men by the carload, and then has them killed and mummified for display in her trophy hall.

Antinea's Arab servant lures three foreign legionnaires to her underground city, where she takes one of them as her lover. She soon tires of him, has him killed and "galvanized" for posterity, then starts in on the second man. He resists her passion, and in her fury at being rebuffed, she drives the third man to murder him.

Feyder's direction was heavy-handed and slow-paced, the acting uneven, and the design over-elaborate and cluttered in a "fussy, quasi-Turkish style." Despite these problems, however, the film was quite successful, and Feyder went on to direct some of the finest films in the history of French cinema. In the U. S., Metro retitled the film **Missing Husbands** (1922).

Although the Atlantis theme has proved to be one of the most popular in literature ever since the 1880s, it has seldom been treated on film. Less than half a dozen filmmakers have tackled the chore of visualizing the Lost Continent, perhaps because of the production expense involved.

The destruction of the Eiffel Tower by redirected lightning, in *La Cite Foudroyee* (*The City Destroyed*) (1923).

Of the films made, at least four have been different versions of this same novel, **L'Atlantide**. Only the 1936 Republic serial, **Undersea Kingdom**, and George Pal's unsuccessful **Atlantis, the Lost Continent** (MGM, 1961), had different storylines.

The definitive version of the Benoit novel was made in 1932 by German director G. W. Pabst. Variously entitled **L'Atlantide, Die Herrin von Atlantis (The Mistress of Atlantis),** and **Lost Atlantis**, this lavish production was filmed with three different casts, in German, French and English. Like the Feyder version, locations included Morocco and Paris; Brigitte Helm, who had played the dual role of woman and robot in **Metropolis**, made a superb Antinea, appearing in all three

The revolt of the masses, in the Russian film *Aelita* (Mezhrabpom, 1924).

versions. Unlike the simpering, emotional Queen in the earlier film, Helm's portrayal is of a coldly imperious woman, beautiful as ice, who delights in destroying men who cannot compete with her. Visually and conceptually, Pabst's film stands as one of the superior romances of the German cinema.

Later attempts at filming the Benoit novel ranged from the ludicrous **Siren of Atlantis** (United Artists, 1947), starring Maria Montez, Jean-Pierre Aumont, and Dennis O'Keefe, to "a tedious travesty," **Journey Beneath the Desert** (a French-Italian co-production, 1961).

Harry Houdini, who had escaped from the critics of his serial **The Master Mystery** in 1918, had by now formed his own film company. Houdini soon showed he wasn't afraid of SF, starring in **The Man from Beyond** (Houdini Pictures Corp., 1921), the story of a super-detective who returns to life after being frozen in Antarctic ice for 100 years. He falls in love with the great-great grand-daughter of his former sweetheart, but he is incarcerated in an insane asylum when he tells his story. He escapes from his solitary cell, where he is held in chains and strait-jacket, and after enough narrow escapes for seven serials, finally succeeds in winning the girl. The climax shows Houdini struggling against the raging currents of Niagara River to save his sweetheart from the brink of the Falls.

SF buffs are accustomed to thinking of 3-D photography as a phenomenon of the '50s, **It Came from Outer Space** (Universal, 1953) being the first SF picture of that period to be filmed in 3-D. But in 1955, while shooting **Forbidden Planet** at MGM, veteran cinematographer George Folsey reminisced: "Incidentally, **Forbidden Planet** is not my first encounter with a science fiction production. 'Way back' in 1922 I photographed a thriller...titled **The Man from Mars**, featuring unearthly creatures with huge heads and gleaming talons. I shot the production in black-and-white in a 'new' process called 3-D!"

But the process wasn't really perfected until much later, and remained an occasional novelty until the '50s, when it suddenly became popular, with dozens of 3-D films jumping off the screens.

Folsey's picture, released as **Radio-Mania** to cash in on the then-current craze for radio (also known as **M. A. R. S.** and **Mars Calling**), was produced by Hodkinson for the Teleview Corpora-tion, and directed by R. William Neil. It starred Grant Mitchell and Margaret Irving in the story of a man who is shown by Martians how to turn coal into diamonds, and clay into gold. Still wary of SF, the producers made the whole thing a dream! Not unexpectedly, "critics praised the effect, if not the merit, of the picture."

A far more interesting concept appeared in a one-reeler produced by John R. Bray in 1922, **The Sky Splitter**. The scenario, by J. A. Norling, who also co-directed with Ashley Miller, dealt with a scientist who journeys to a strange planet in a winged rocket ship that goes faster than light. There he is able to receive light from earth, and resolve it to show events that occurred 100 years before he left. He also views his own childhood and relives the past 50 years of his life.

Although treated in a comic manner, this was the first screen version of a faster-than-light spaceship, later to become a stock cliche of written SF during the heyday of the pulp magazines.

France took the lead in SF film production in 1923. Luitz-Marat produced and directed a serial disaster film in which a madman with a "thunderbolt" ray machine captures and redirects lightning to destroy Paris. **La Cite Foudroyee (The City Destroyed)** has some spectacular footage of the Eiffel Tower collapsing under a barrage of fiery bolts, with Paris in ruins.

That same year, Marcel L'Herbier co-wrote and directed **L'Inhumaine (The Inhuman One)**, a slight but curious story of an opera singer (Eve Francis) who treats all her lovers with disdain until she is poisoned by a jealous maharajah. She is then brought back from the dead in a danger-ous experiment conducted by her lover, an engineer. The value of this film lies not in its story, nor in the typically remote, frigid direction of L'Herbier, but in its striking art direction. The sets were designed in the cubist style by architect Robert Mallet-Stevens and the painter Fernand Leger, assisted by Claude Autant-Lara and Alberto Cavalcanti; their influence can be seen in **Metropolis** three years later. Rounding out this incredible array of European talent was Darius Milhaud, who composed the score for the film.

A more light-hearted film was **Paris Qui Dort (Paris Asleep)** (1923) written, directed, and edited by the great French director Rene Clair. Also known as **The Invisible Ray** or **The Crazy Ray**, this delightful film, with its trick effects and flashes of sharp wit, was Clair's affectionate tribute to Melies and his era.

A young nightwatchman (Albert Prejean) assigned to the top of the Eiffel Tower wakes up one morning to discover that all of Paris has been frozen into immobility—time has been stopped. Descending from the Tower, the young man wanders through the streets of Paris, observing such

The dinosaur attacks, in Harry Hoyt's *The Lost World* (First National, 1925).

bizarre scenes as a thief and the pursuing policeman both frozen in mid-stride, and a dustman caught in the act of emptying a bin. He discovers other people untouched by the freeze, who are behaving in disreputable fashion, getting drunk and fighting over the only girl left unfrozen. A radio message leads them to the house of Dr. Bardin, amiable and dreamy, whose machine has broadcast the ray that caused the disaster. It was all unintentional, and Dr. Bardin finally thinks of turning off the machine, restoring Paris to normal.

The Last Man on Earth (Fox, 1924) showed the beginnings of Hollywood's cautious willingness to attempt a few SF subjects. In the future of 1954, a strange disease kills off all the male population over 14—except one (Earle Fox). Women take over the government, and two female senators compete for the hero's attentions. This idea was later to become the basis for a number of comic SF novels, most notably Pat Frank's **Mr. Adam** (1946). The film was remade in 1933 as a musical comedy called **It's Great to Be Alive**.

The Russians tried a couple of SF film experiments about this time, finding in the genre an excellent means of expressing their revolutionary doctrines. **Aelita** (Mezhrabpom, 1924), directed by Jacob Protazanov, was based on a novel by Alexei Tolstoi, and tells the story of the first Russian cosmonauts, engineers Los and Gusev, who journey to Mars in a spaceship. There they discover a beautiful world, but one whose society is in the throes of a savage class war. The Martian workers are controlled by the capitalistic Martian aristocracy, who force the workers to wear black box helmets that monitor their thoughts. Los falls in love with the beautiful princess Aelita, but Gusev, who had been a soldier of the Revolution, leads the masses in revolt against their tyrannical masters.

The film was less notable for its propaganda than for the striking cubist art design, strong groupings of crowd scenes, spectacular sets, and grotesque costuming. The film was so popular in Russia that a short animated parody of it was produced in 1924 entitled **Mezhplanetnaya Revolutsiya (Interplanetary Revolution).**

A second Russian SF film followed in 1925, based on a novel by Alexei Tolstoi, **The Hyperloid of Engineer Garin** (later published in English as **The Garin Death Ray**). It was called simply **Loutch Smerti (The Death Ray)**, and was directed by Lev Kuleshov from a scenario by the great Russian director V. I. Pudovkin, who also assisted in the art direction, served as assistant director on the film, and acted in it as well!

This melodrama about an inventor whose laser-like death ray is coveted by anti-revolutionary powers is set in an "unnamed Western country," and the hero uses the device to protect his home city from Facist bomb raids. The technical excellence of both this film and **Aelita** showed that the Russians were second to none in filmmaking technique, although the predictably large amounts of propaganda in the pictures' story lines kept them from being superior examples of SF cinema.

By far the most significant SF film of 1925 came from Hollywood. **The Lost World** (First National) was based on the 1912 novel by Arthur Conan Doyle, and was directed by Harry Hoyt. Wallace Beery, as Doyle's cantankerous scientist-explorer, Professor Challenger, leads an expedition to a plateau deep in the South American jungle, where prehistoric monsters still roam and do battle, just as they did millions of years ago. After many hair-raising adventures, including a volcanic eruption, and an attack by a super-human ape-man (Bull Montana), the party captures a disabled Brontosaurus and takes it back to London for exhibition. Once there, however, it breaks loose and smashes up a good part of London before escaping down the Thames and out to sea.

The film, whose cast also included Bessie Love, Lewis Stone, Lloyd Hughes, and Arthur Hoyt, contained several tinted sequences, and the special effects were strikingly produced by Fred Jackman and Willis O'Brien, who created 49 miniature dinosaurs, animated by his assistant,

Two scenes from *Metropolis* (Ufa, 1926): (above) The "Pater Noster Machine"; (below) a panoramic view of the soulless city of tomorrow.

(above)   Karl Freund sets up a shot with Gustav Frohlich in front of the great dial;   (below) Maria tries to save the children as *Metropolis* is flooded.

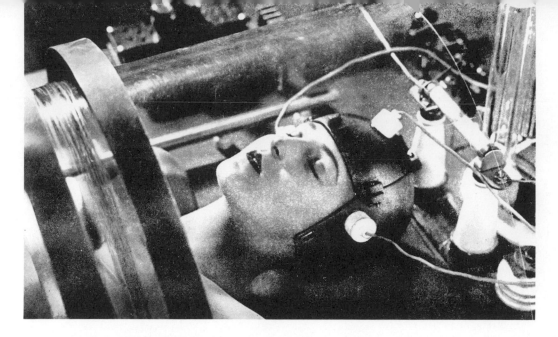

Having been kidnapped by Rotwang, Maria (Brigitte Helm) is used by the scientist to transform his robot into a perfect likeness of the girl (*Metropolis*, Ufa, 1926).

Marcel Delgado. Even though somewhat crude and jerky by today's standards, the dinosaurs stole the show, and set the stage for many monster films to come. Later attempts at model animation have improved the movements, but they are still only refinements of the basic processes pioneered by O'Brien. **The Lost World** was very popular in its time and remains a favorite today whenever shown; it was a warm-up exercise for O'Brien and Delgado, who were to become famous eight years later for their work in another variation of the same story, **King Kong**.

The addition of color and CinemaScope did nothing to improve the disappointingly mediocre remake of **The Lost World** (Twentieth Century-Fox, 1960). Claude Rains was sadly miscast as Professor Challenger, and Michael Rennie looked like he would rather be somewhere else in the galaxy. Even Jill St. John couldn't distract from the phony Technicolor vegetation, and the tired old trick of substituting tricked-up lizards and iguanas for stop-motion dinosaurs.

In 1926, only one SF film worthy of note was produced—but that one is a true classic, the first great achievement of the SF cinema—Fritz Lang's **Metropolis** (Ufa). The screenplay by Lang and his wife, Thea von Harbou, was based on the latter's novel and is set—although it is never specified—in about the year 2000 A. D. Metropolis is a gigantic city divided into two distinct divisions—a luxurious upper class who enjoy exotic pleasures above ground, and a working class who live beneath the city in slums, slaving away at the dials and furnaces of the great machines that power Metropolis. The ruler of this vast domain is Joh Frederson (Alfred Abel), a man with enormous responsibilities. His young son, Freder, (Gustav Frohlich) becomes curious about the workers below, but his father is too preoccupied and evasive to satisfy him. A brief glimpse of a beautiful girl named Maria (Brigitte Helm), and her charge of ragged children, sends Freder down into the underground levels to search for her.

Dressed in the anonymous coveralls of the workers, Freder mingles with the workers, and sees for the first time the horrors of life below: the monstrous "Pater Noster Machine," which resembles a hideous idol demanding human sacrifice; the trudging defeated men, exhausting themselves at meaningless tasks, moving dials, jiggling levers, and opening valves amid a steam-filled Hell. When a worker collapses at a huge thermometer gauge, Freder takes over for him to prevent an explosion, but is soon reduced to near-exhaustion himself. He barely makes it through the terrible ten-hour shift before being relieved by a fresh worker, and then finds his way at last to Maria, who preaches to the slaves of the machine in a crude church. To Freder, Maria's voice is like "the amen of God," as she retells the story of the Tower of Babel, preaching in parable form the necessity for mediation between labor and management.

Wishing to crush any possible rebellion, the Master of Metropolis enlists the help of scientist cum black magician Rotwang (Rudolf Klein-Rogge), one of the screen's most memorable villains, with his artificial hand of dark, glistening material. He shows Frederson his crowning achievement—the coldly beautiful female robot who is one of the finest images in all SF cinema. Frederson orders Rotwang to transform the robot into the likeness of Maria, so that it can take her place and spread confusion among the workers, destroying their confidence in her.

Rotwang kidnaps Maria and takes her to his laboratory where, in a superbly-designed sequence that has yet to be matched for sheer visual power by any SF or horror film, he clothes the metal maiden with synthetic flesh in the exact image of Maria. Her movements jerky at first, her eyes glaring evil, the robot is a cruel parody of the ethereal Maria, and it is a tribute to the acting skill of Brigitte Helm that she makes the transition so believable.

The "new" Maria, now wickedly seductive, incites the workers to destroy the dikes and machines, but in so doing they flood their own homes. Furious, they turn on the robot, and burn her at the stake, but she only laughs horribly as the flames scar her metal body harmlessly. The real Maria escapes from Rotwang's house, and manages to lead many of the children to safety as the now maddened workers run through the city in full rebellion, smashing the machines in a spectacular climax of destruction.

Rotwang tries to kill Maria on the rooftops, but Freder comes to her rescue, and hurls the mad scientist to his death. Then, with Maria's help, Freder manages to calm the workers, and reach an understanding between them and his father, the Master of Metropolis. Frederson, aghast at the havoc his unfeeling attitude has caused, finally agrees that "there can be no understanding between the hands and the brain unless the heart acts as mediator."

The influences of such films as **Homunculus, L'Inhumaine, Aelita,** and **Caligari** are apparent in this film, but Lang brings it all together into an original and powerful vision of his own. The atmosphere and visual style of this film were to influence the concept of virtually every filmic portrayal of the future for many years to come. In addition, the technical innovations of its special effects, involving models, mirrors, and forced perspective were quickly absorbed into world

A television phone, from Elvey's *High Treason* (Gaumont, 1929) the first talking picture made in Great Britain.

cinema technology.

In terms of content, however, criticism of **Metropolis** was sharply divided. H. G. Wells, for instance, perhaps personally piqued because his own visions had not yet seen adequate expression on the screen, condemned it as "quite the silliest film," and felt that Lang's conception was an immature and superficial one, without knowledge of society or science.

Lang himself had said that he didn't much care for the film after he had finished it, although he loved it while making it. He also felt that the message of the heart mediating between labor and management was perhaps too simplistic; but later, more positive reactions from new generations of filmgoers, particularly the young, softened his views somewhat.

One reason the film was not so well received in America and England was that it had been drastically cut by the playwright Channing Pollock and others from its original 17 reels down to ten. This condensed version, lacking much important connecting material, is unfortunately the only one that survives today, and even it is often cut down further to about 90 minutes.

Despite the naivete of its concept, the expert showmanship, fertile imagination, and technical and artistic excellence of **Metropolis** give it a firm place in SF film history—the culmination to that time of the visions begun with Melies.

Brigitte Helm, fresh from her triumph in **Metropolis**, starred in another German SF film for Ufa in 1927, but this one was destined for oblivion. Perhaps this was because it was a "passionate appeal for world peace," a concept unpopular with the German psyche, which was still smarting from the defeat of 1918. **Am Rande der Welt (At the Edge of the World)** was a future war film of the type so prevalent back in the Teens, written and directed by Karl Grune. The film is notable for its design, by A. D. Neppach, and for the fact that it featured young Wilhelm (William) Dieterle, who was later to become one of Hollywood's finest directors.

Another French director who, like Rene Clair, dabbled briefly and lightly in SF before going on to other things, was Jean Renoir. His fourth film was **Sur un Air de Charleston (Charleston)** (1927), a futuristic comedy set in the year 2028, when Europe and America have been covered by another Ice Age. A black explorer (Johnny Higgins) flies from Central Africa, where civilization now flourishes, to visit Europe, then thought uninhabited. Amid an elaborate set depicting the ruins of Paris, he discovers a "primitive" girl (Catherine Hessling), a blonde savage dancing the Charleston. Her "strange native dance" captivates the explorer, and he takes her back with him to Africa. The dance craze of the '20s has outlasted even the end of European civilization!

This 22-minute divertissement was Renoir's homage to Melies, as **Paris Qui Dort** was Clair's. Unlike Clair, however, Renoir later returned to SF as a means of expressing his ideas about the necessity of rehumanizing and revitalizing the cold humorlessness of scientists. **Le Testament du Docteur Cordelier** (1959) starred Jean-Louis Barrault in the double role of a modern Jekyll and Hyde. A third film, **Le Dejeuner sur L'Herbe** (1959), better known as **Picnic on the Grass**, is set in a future when all of man's problems have been solved. Both were made for French TV.

Meanwhile, back in Germany, Brigitte Helm was again playing the kind of soulless vamp she seemed to portray so well. **Alraune** (also known as **Unholy Love**) (Ufa, 1928) was based on the popular 1911 German novel by Hanns Heinz Ewers, and was written and directed by Henrik Galeen, by now an expert in German horror films.

A scientist (Paul Wegener), experimenting with artificial insemination, creates a woman without a soul, the daughter of a hanged man and a prostitute. She is named "Alraune," after the legendary mandrake root with supposedly magical powers. The soulless child grows to adulthood, and learns the secret of her birth by reading her creator's diary. She realizes what she is, but cannot control her amoral nature, bringing ruin to lover after lover; she finally destroys herself, the

The explorers on the Moon, in *Die Frau im Mond* (*The Woman in the Moon*) (Ufa, 1929).

female counterpart of Homunculus.

Once again, German filmmakers had hit upon a perfect expression of the feelings of frustration and inferiority in the German soul. The measure of **Alraune**'s popularity is the number of times it has been filmed. Two earlier versions had already been made in 1918, one in Germany and one in Hungary, directed by Mihaly Kertesz (later known in Hollywood as Michael Curtiz); but the Galeen version remains the definitive one.

A later version was made as a talking picture in 1930, again starring Brigitte Helm, but with a different supporting cast, and directed by Richard Oswald, whose first foray into SF had been **The Arc**, back in 1919. This version was also known as **Daughter of Evil**, and had a musical score by Bronislaw Kaper. **Alraune** was remade once again in 1952, as **Unnatural** (DCA), starring Hildegarde Neff and Erich von Stroheim.

35

Fritz Lang followed up his earlier success with another SF picture for Ufa in 1929, **Die Frau im Mond (The Woman in the Moon)**. It had already begun production when mechanically-recorded speech and sound effects finally became realities for films, but Lang (perhaps unwisely) decided to go ahead with a silent version. Like **Metropolis, Die Frau im Mond** was directed and co-written by Lang from a novel by Thea von Harbou.

A professor (Klaus Pohl) has perfected a space ship to reach the Moon, which he is convinced contains large quantities of gold. However, he has been unable to obtain financing for his dream, and years of frustration have made him almost a madman. Finally, a wealthy young assistant (Willy Fritsch) is able to secure backing from a secret council of businessmen who are determined to acquire the gold for their own interests. They select one of their number (Fritz Rasp) to accompany the expedition, and "protect" the gold shipment.

After a number of attempts to destroy the rocket, it blasts off for the Moon in a spectacular launch sequence. The crew consists of the professor and his assistant, the businessman "watchdog," an engineer (Gustav von Wagenheim), and two stowaways: the engineer's fiancee (Gerda Maurus), and a young boy who is a SF fan (Gustl Stark-Gstettenbauer). Naturally, a love triangle develops between the girl, the engineer, and the young assistant.

After experiencing acceleration and weightlessness, the explorers land safely on the dark side of the Moon, which they discover has oxygen, and set out to explore the terrain. The professor, who has now become quite mad, discovers the gold deposits he dreamed were there, but the business representative follows him, and causes him to fall to his death in a crater. The boy and the engineer witness the crime, and a fight occurs back at the ship. The villain is killed, but not before he releases half the ship's air supply, which makes it necessary for one person to remain on the Moon so that the others may return to Earth. The assistant volunteers, but the engineer drugs him and sends him and the boy home on automatic control. The engineer and the girl remain on the Moon's bleak surface, hoping that some day they will be rescued.

Although strong on visual effects, **Die Frau im Mond** is a disappointing and unworthly successor to **Metropolis**. The elaborate staging of the rocket's launch, with the surging crowds and searchlights, is visually impressive, as is the interior of the rocket, and the depiction of weight-

The advanced city of tomorrow, as depicted by Maurice Elvey in his film, *High Treason* (Gaumont, 1929).

lessness. The surface of the Moon is less successful, but this is largely because of the increased knowledge we have today of the real conditions on the Moon. It is hard to suppress a chuckle at the sight of people running around the Lunar surface in ordinary clothes, breathing an atmosphere (which doesn't seem to affect the traditional black Lunar sky filled with stars), and experiencing no effect of reduced gravitation. All of this, combined with overacting, and the turgid melodrama of the plot, dim the film considerably. It represents no significant advance over **Metropolis**, made five years previous.

Nevertheless, the film has an important place in SF film history as the last major silent picture to be made, and the first to attempt a realistic portrayal of space travel. Turning away from the fantasy conceptions of Melies, and other early interplanetary films, Lang secured the best technical advisors he could find: Willy Ley, later to become a well-known popularizer of science in America, and Dr. Hermann Oberth, the noted rocket expert, who designed the space ship.

The film's influence on later cinematic Moon voyages is incalculable; it is particularly evident in George Pal's **Destination Moon** (1950). But Lang's influence was more immediately felt on a **Metropolis**-like forecast of life in 1940, **High Treason** (Gaumont, 1929), directed by Maurice Elvey, and starring Benita Hume, Raymond Massey, and Rene Ray, who also authored several SF novels. Based on a play by Pemberton Billing, this first British talking picture was a hodge-podge of ideas, from earlier films of future aerial wars, through **Aelita** and **Metropolis**. Unfortunately, the ideas didn't mesh very well; although there are some interesting depictions of giant newscreens, television-phones, helitaxis, and a tunnel under the English Channel, the film lacks coherence. As one historian has noted, "**High Treason**, with its arts-and-crafts design by Andrew Mazzei, revealed only too clearly how poorly England produces a film of this kind."

In Elvey's 1940, a war is in progress between the "Federated Atlantic States" and the "United States of Europe." A sequence showing the gas-bombing of New York got the film banned in that city!

The last major SF effort of the '20s was to point the way toward the technical future of the SF film; prophetically, it was produced in Hollywood, which was at last to take the lead in SF films in the '30s, '40s, and '50s.

Recalling the success of his 1916 version of Jules Verne's **20,000 Leagues Under the Sea**, J. E. Williamson came to MGM in 1925 to work on a film of Verne's sequel, **The Mysterious Island**. But aside from the title, Lucien Hubbard's screenplay utilized nothing of Verne except the submarine (actually, two) and the use of Captain Nemo's real name, Count Dakkar (here demoted from Prince), for Lionel Barrymore's crusty old scientist. Three directors received credit: Lucien Hubbard, Maurice Tourneur, and Benjamin Christiansen.

Captain Nemo (Lionel Barrymore), in *The Mysterious Island* (MGM, 1925).

Portions of the film were shot in primitive two-strip Technicolor, and several sequences had sound effects and (faked) dialogue. Although crudely done, it was the first SF film to utilize both color and sound, and pointed the way for the more imaginative use of these elements in later SF films.

The production was plagued with technical problems: filming began in 1926, but was not completed until 1929, due to the decision to include sound sequences for commercial appeal, and because of the destruction by a hurricane of the second unit, shooting near the Bahamas in 1927. These and other problems brought the total production costs to over two million dollars.

In his secret laboratory, Dakkar invents an advanced type of submarine with which to explore the ocean floor. He believes that a half-human, half-fish race lives in the depths, because of a small skeleton he has brought up. But Russian agents want the underwater craft for war purposes, and attack the island stronghold. While Dakkar is being tortured, his sister Sonia (Jane Daly), and her sweetheart Nikolai (Lloyd Hughes) are exploring underwater. When they surface, they are fired upon by the Russians, and the ship is damaged. It sinks down to the fathoms-deep ocean floor, where a strange undersea civilization is revealed, peopled by bizarre little fish-men with glowing eyes, a giant octopus, and sea dragons.

Falon (Montagu Love), the villainous Russian leader, seeing that Dakkar will reveal nothing under torture, commandeers the second submarine and heads for the depths. After driving off a sea monster, Nikolai and his crew win the friendship of the little people, who finally mete out to Falon a grisly death.

When they return to the surface, Nikolai and Sonia discover a dying Count Dakkar, who executes his "curious last will and testament."

As is so often the case, the special effects are overshadowed by the absurdly melodramatic story, but the care lavished on the underwater scenes, with the eerie masses of tiny, glowing-eyed people, the battles with aqueous monsters, and the slow, dream-like movements of men in diving suits, makes the film well worth seeing in one of its rare revivals today.

Four other versions of **The Mysterious Island** have been made, one of them a serial (1951), and another a Russian film (1941); but only the 1961 Columbia version, directed by Cy Enfield, is worthy of note. Here again, although more faithful to the novel, the story is barely adequate; but its visual interest is maintained by the addition of giant beasts and insects, animated by Ray Harryhausen, which attack the castaways on the island. The sequence where giant bees trap two of the humans in a huge honeycomb is superb. Herbert Lom is an adequate Captain Nemo, but one wishes that James Mason had been available once again.

The last year of the 1920s had seen the coming of sound and color to motion pictures—science fiction had finally learned to talk. The ravages of the Depression would soon cause a deep hunger for escapist cinema—and what could fill the bill better than science fiction? Many of the best European directors were coming to Hollywood to pour the rich fruits of their experience into the industry, and the stage was set for a decade of fascinating and spectacular achievements in SF filmmaking. Even though it would be largely eclipsed and dominated by the burgeoning horror film genre, the SF film was to survive for two decades as a significant and colorful screen sub-genre, until its triumphant renaissance in the 1950s. **Metropolis** had finally crystallized the promise inherent in Melies's early productions; and the best years of SF cinema were still to come.

SERIALS AND SCIENTISTS
(1930–1949)

The first SF film of the new decade was also the first SF musical, with songs by DeSylva, Brown, and Henderson. **Just Imagine** (Fox) was a lavish extravaganza of New York in 1980, a time when people have numbers instead of names, and food comes out of machines in the form of pills. Directed by David Butler, who also collaborated on the script with the three composers, the story line concerns J-21 (John Garrick), a young transatlantic pilot, and his sweetheart, LN-18 (Maureen O'Sullivan), who want to get married; but such things are now decided by a marriage tribunal, and LN-18 is pledged to a wealthy publisher, MT-3 (Kenneth Thomson). However, J-21 is given a probationary period to prove his worthiness. He meets a scientist, X-10 (Wilfred Lucas), who has just revived a man from 1930 who was supposedly killed by lightning, but instead has been unconscious for 50 years. The sleeper (El Brendel) is assigned the name "Single-O," and J-21 and his pal, RT-42 (Frank Albertson), proceed to show him the sights of this brave new world. After some amusing reactions from Single-O, they meet another scientist, Z-4 (Hobart Bosworth), who has perfected an interplanetary rocket. J-21 agrees to fly the rocket to Mars to prove himself worthy of LN-18 and does so, accompanied by RT-42 and Single-O.

The two lovers, J-21 (John Garrick) and LN-18 (Maureen O'Sullivan) from *Just Imagine* (Fox, 1930).

On Mars, they find a primitive civilization of humans ruled over by a queen named Loo-Loo, who has an evil double named Boo-Boo (both played by Joyzelle)—in fact, all the Martians have doubles, one good, one bad. After a great deal of silly running around, Single-O rescues his buddies from jail, where they have been tossed by the bad Queen. They escape back to the rocket, bringing a Martian with them to prove they made the journey, and J-21 is a hero. The court rules in his favor and he gets to marry LN-18 in the best tradition of Hollywood musical hokum.

The wedding of the musical, then enormously popular with film audiences, with the SF film might have worked, had the basic material been better. But the good gags are few and far between, and after the novelty of the setting has worn off (well before the picture is half over), the rest must be endured rather than enjoyed. The level of humor in general makes the Three Stooges look like Woody Allen, especially during the Martian sequence. Sample dialogue: ''I'm going to Mars!'' ''You're crazy—you're going to bed.'' Single-O's reaction to his first view of Mars: ''So this is Mars—we have a spot like this three miles from my home.''

Nevertheless, the picture remains worth seeing (once) for the SF film buff, because of the impressive but all too brief scenes of the **Metropolis**-like city of 1980 from the air. As the two lovers talk to each other from air-cars hovering over the 200-storey skyscrapers of tomorrow's New York, great expectations are raised in the viewer which are all too soon dispelled. The revival scene in the laboratory of X-10 is well done, and the rocket ship, which served as the prototype for Flash Gordon's ship six years later, is a nice nostalgic touch when the film is seen today. The rest is sadly lacking in imagination. Footage from this film, especially shots of the futuristic city, have often been used in other films, as in the 1939 Universal serial, **Buck Rogers**.

In 1931, the immediate and enormous success of Universal's two horror classics, **Dracula** and **Frankenstein**, transplanted the long and carefully cultivated aesthetics of the German horror film to Hollywood, and a cycle of blood-chilling cinema shockers was born. Tod Browning and James Whale—and later, Val Lewton—emerged as the premier directors, with Boris Karloff and Bela Lugosi as the principal stars. Audiences couldn't get enough of these pictures, and the studios churned out vast numbers of them over the next two decades; most are pretty awful, but there remains an impressive core of classics.

The result of this horror boom was the temporary disappearance of SF films as a separate genre; however, individual movies would still emerge from time to time cloaked and masked as supernatural cinema. SF remained more clearly identifiable in the serial, which became more popular than ever with sound. Robots, death rays, and other superscientific gadgets abounded, and comic strip and pulp magazine characters joined en masse in the hunt for the inevitably hooded villains. In fact, the '30s saw the advent of the first real SF serials, **The Phantom Empire** (Mascot, 1935), and **Undersea Kingdom** (Republic, 1936), closely followed by the more famous Flash Gordon epics.

Six Hours to Live (Fox, 1932), directed by William Dieterle, was an atypical example of SF disguised as a crime melodrama, rather than an out-and-out horror film. Warner Baxter starred as a murdered diplomat brought back to life for six hours by a special ray. He brings the murderer to justice, then destroys the ray before dying for the second and final time.

This same basic idea was more fun as a true horror film, in the hands of director Michael Curtiz and Boris Karloff. **The Walking Dead** (Warner Bros., 1936) was a fine example of SF with a fright wig, as Karloff is brought back from the dead in Edmund Gwenn's laboratory, then shambles out to bring retribution to the crooks who framed him for murder, causing his execution.

Karloff, fresh from his triumph in **Frankenstein**, also appeared as a superbly-made-up Fu Manchu in the best of the many films based on Sax Rohmer's popular Devil Doctor. Directed by

Charles Brabin and Charles Vidor, **The Mask of Fu Manchu** (MGM, 1932) was produced by an uncredited Irving Thalberg, and splendidly designed by Cedric Gibbons. Sparing no evil trick to secure the legendary sword and mask of Genghis Khan, which will establish his power over the "teeming hordes of Asia," and make him ruler of the world, Fu Manchu is thwarted by Nayland Smith (Lewis Stone), Professor von Berg (Jean Hersholt), and young Terry Granville (Charles Starrett). After subjecting these stalwarts to kidnapping and torture, and aided by his lovely but evil daughter, Fah Lo See (Myrna Loy), Fu Manchu obtains the true mask and sword. The scene in his laboratory with sparks flying from his machines as he tests the sword is worthy of James Whale. He then sentences Smith and von Berg to death in a crocodile pit, and a gleaming spiked vise, respectively, while Granville is destined to become a slave to Fah Lo See. But the heroes escape, and destroy Fu Manchu with his own death ray.

Two scenes from *The Mask of Fu Manchu* (MGM, 1932), directed by Charles Brabin and Charles Vidor from Sax Rohmer's novel: (left) Boris Karloff as Fu Manchu; (below) Karloff displays the legendary sword of Genghis Khan, which will make him ruler of the world.

Lota, the Panther-Girl (Kathleen Burke), menaces two visitors to the *Island of Lost Souls* (Paramount, 1932), based on Wells's novel, *The Island of Dr. Moreau*.

This is a true example of SF as horror film: the bad doctor's devices are strictly superscientific—not a werewolf in sight—but everything is played for shock and suspense. Karloff portrays Fu Manchu with consummate artistry—just the right touch of humor—and his delicately lisped English ("I was educated at Oxford, you know") is superbly sinister.

Although the "Golden Age" of film in Germany was now over, with many directors and writers sensing the forthcoming loss of freedom, and coming to America (Fritz Lang was to immigrate in 1934 after being told by Goebbels that Hitler wanted him to make Nazi propaganda films), occasional SF films of interest still appeared. One such was **F.P. 1** (Ufa/Gaumont/Fox, 1932), co-written by Kurt (Curt) Siodmak from his novel, **F. P. 1 Antwortet Nicht (F. P. 1 Does Not Reply)**. Like many European films of the period, three simultaneous versions were shot for French, German, and English release, all with different casts. The English version starred Conrad Veidt, the French version, Charles Boyer, and the German version, matinee idol Hans Albers and Peter Lorre. Direction was by Karl Hartl.

Chief engineer-pilot Albers is encouraged to construct a floating aerodrome in the middle of the Atlantic Ocean. He does so, and Floating Platform No. 1, a futuristic island of steel and glass, becomes a way-station to enable huge airliners to achieve transcontinental flight. But foreign powers wish to see the platform destroyed: saboteurs gas the maintenance crew and open the compressed air tanks that keep F. P. 1 afloat. The attempt is foiled, however, and all ends happily.

Once again, the technology and visuals are the most impressive aspects of this film. The aerodrome was designed by Erich Kettelhut, with technical advice from Dr. Albert Henninger, and was superbly photographed by Gunter Rittau, who had masterminded the process photography for **Metropolis**. Scenes of the platform under construction and of great tri-motor airliners landing on its metal surface were much more exciting to SF fans than Siodmak's mediocre plot, even though the advent of long-range aircraft was soon to make his concept obsolete.

Back in Hollywood, a superior blend of SF and horror was finally achieved in **Island of Lost Souls** (Paramount, 1932), directed by Erle Kenton from a screenplay by Waldemar Young and Philip Wylie. Based on H. G. Wells's 1896 novel, **The Island of Dr. Moreau**, Paramount found in this horrifying tale of a mad scientist experimenting with surgical transformations of animals into men all the elements for a good batch of chills.

After waiting so long to see another of his SF works on the screen, Wells was reportedly disappointed with this effort, perhaps because of his sympathies with the strong anti-vivisectionist movement in Britain at the time. "The House of Pain" was a bit much for British sensibilities, and the film was banned there, as well as in New Zealand, and some Midwestern American states.

Wells's disapproval is unfortunate, because the film is a classic of SF horror, exceptionally well-made, with an air of evil and degeneracy throughout. Charles Laughton brought a new dimension to the role of the mad scientist, with his cool, suave portrayal of god-like power and flashes of brutal sadism. Kathleen Burke supplies a savage eroticism as Lota, the Panther-Girl, and Bela Lugosi as The Sayer of the Law is excellent in his hairy makeup. The monstrous "manimals" are believably horrendous, and the ghastly climax, when they gang up on Moreau and begin to perform unthinkable surgery on him in the House of Pain, is almost too much to bear.

A new version of the Wells novel, under its original title, has just been released at this writing, with Burt Lancaster as Dr. Moreau. It will have to go a long way to beat **Island of Lost Souls.**

The beast people confront Dr. Moreau (Charles Laughton) in *Island of Lost Souls* (Paramount, 1932).

Wells was better satisfied with the next film made from his fiction, **The Invisible Man** (Universal, 1933). This 1897 tale of a scientist who turns himself invisible with a drug that also drives him mad proved a superb vehicle for the expressive direction of James Whale (**Frankenstein, The Old Dark House**), and for the equally superb special effects of John P. Fulton. Here, although the horror aspects of the situation are stressed, the SF element dominates, and the screenplay, by R. C. Sherriff and Philip Wylie (both SF authors) is literate and sprinkled with dark humor.

In his first screen performance, much of which is achieved by voice alone, Claude Rains plays Griffin, who takes refuge in a small English village while he tries to discover an antidote to the

A very rare production still from James Whale's *The Invisible Man* (Universal, 1933), based on H. G. Wells's novel of the same name.

drug that has made him invisible. Hounded by curious villagers, he succumbs to madness and forces his ex-colleague to help inaugurate a vengeful reign of terror. Murders, train-wrecks, and mental harassment are his weapons, and not even the love of his sweetheart (Gloria Stuart) can save him. Eventually, he is traced to a hay-filled barn in a snow-covered farmyard, and the police, whom he has made fools of throughout the film, set fire to his refuge. He runs out into the snow, but his footprints appear clearly, giving the police an approximate target. They shoot, and the Invisible Man falls at last. Only when he dies in the hospital does he return to visibility.

Whale's direction, the excellent script, Rains's fine performance, and most of all, the ingeniously believable special effects (the scene in which Rains unbandages his head, bit by bit, to reveal nothingness, is unforgettable), make this film one of the finest contributions to both the SF and horror film genres.

The success of **The Invisible Man** spawned a host of inferior sequels, from such early efforts as **The Invisible Man Returns** (Universal, 1939), co-written by Curt Siodmak and starring Vincent Price as the invisible brother of the original Invisible Man; to **The Invisible Man's Revenge** (Universal, 1944), in which Jon Hall is forced to give the original formula he had rediscovered to a

(above) Claude Rains, *The Invisible Man*, shares a tender moment with Gloria Stuart. Ironically, Rains, in his first screen performance, is not actually seen by the viewer until the end of the film.

(above right) *The Invisible Man Returns* (Universal, 1939) featured Vincent Price as the shadowy brother of Claude Rains; here, Cobb (Sir Cedric Hardwicke) awakens to find the Invisible Man leveling a gun at him.

(right) In *The Invisible Woman* (Universal, 1940), Kitty (Virginia Bruce) drinks alcohol to become invisible, thereby saving Professor Gibbs (John Barrymore).

criminal bent on revenge; through **Abbott and Costello Meet the Invisible Man** (Universal, 1951); various little-known Mexican, Turkish, and German versions; and a recent ill-fated television series starring David McCallum.

In between, other invisible persons also appeared on the screen: **The Invisible Woman** (Universal, 1940), in which John Barrymore's machine made Virginia Bruce invisible so she could hunt spies; and **Invisible Agent** (Universal, 1942), another Curt Siodmak story, again starring Jon Hall, this time pitted against Nazi agents Cedric Hardwicke and Peter Lorre.

Although none of these films dealt with Wells's original characters, most of them retained the credit line ''suggested by the novel of H. G. Wells.'' By now he must have washed his hands of the whole thing, and written it off as another loss.

Two scenes from *Deluge* (RKO, 1933): (below) New York is split asunder by a giant earthquake; (right) Manhattan disappears beneath the waves.

As a matter of fact, invisibility in films was nothing new in 1933: more than 35 films have been listed with the word "invisible" in the title, most of them dealing with some process for making a human being vanish. It was used as a favorite device in the early comedies and serials. The earliest known invisibility film is **Les Invisibles** (also known as **Invisible Thief**), a French film directed for Pathe by Gaston Velle and Gabriel Moreau in 1905. The self-doomed Invisible Man remains the most popular single character created by Wells, and one of the most memorable in SF cinema.

Men Must Fight (MGM, 1933) is a little-known future film set in a 1940 torn by a new world war. Prophecies of this kind were beginning to gather some steam once again, as events in Europe began to trouble the world; and this film, though much less spectacular, is an interesting predecessor to the much more famous **Things to Come** (1936). Directed by Edgar Selwyn, and photographed by George Folsey of early 3-D fame, the film was a plea for sanity, with Diana Wynyard leading a peace crusade in vain—New York is bombed and the Empire State Building destroyed.

This film and the next one discussed are also interesting examples of the beginning re-emergence of the SF picture as a separate genre, freed from the Gothic influence of the horror film. Nineteen thirty-three was proving to be a banner year for SF cinema, and the best was yet to come!

The announcement of **Deluge** (RKO, 1933) was a delightful surprise for long-suffering SF film fans—a true SF spectacle, based on the novel by British author S. Fowler Wright. But alas, the film did not live up to expectations. Little of Wright's story except the title and the idea of a great flood remained, and even that was localized in New York City. The maudlin, soap-opera plot had none of the sweep and grandeur of the early end-of-the-world epics: terrible disaster for New York is forecast by Professor Carlysle (Edward Van Sloan), but no one listens. Sure enough, the entire city is soon destroyed by a gigantic earthquake, and Manhattan Island is inundated by a huge tidal wave. Martin Webster (Sidney Blackmer) survives the disaster, but believes that his wife and children are dead. Forty miles from the ruins of the city, Webster meets and falls in love with pretty Claire Arlington (Peggy Shannon). After some tedious conflict with a villain named Jephson (Fred Kohler), the lovers discover (surprise!) that Webster's wife (Lois Wilson) and children are still alive and well! Claire, of course, does the right thing. "She leaves Webster to his family and swims off."

Nevertheless, the film made an indelible impression on all those who were fortunate enough to see it in 1933. The spectacular New York destruction scenes and the giant tidal wave occur at the beginning of the film, and while not completely convincing (the models look too much like models, and the water is sometimes out of focus), they paved the way for catastrophe films to come. A direct influence can be seen in George Pal's 1951 film, **When Worlds Collide**, in which New York is again inundated.

The miniatures were handled by Ned Mann, who was later to perfect his craft in **Things to Come**; he called them "the largest, and certainly the most intricate job of miniature work ever done in any production." Unfortunately, the film has been lost to modern audiences, as RKO sold the destruction sequences to Republic, who used them in many cheapie serials and features, including **S. O. S. Tidal Wave** (1939), an otherwise undistinguished film.

Melies's 1907 vision of a tunnel beneath the English Channel had been revived briefly in 1914 as war jitters prompted the production of a British film called **The Great German North Sea Tunnel** (Dreadnaught), in which the tunnel was seen as an underground invasion route. But it was a German author, Bernhard Kellermann, whose novel **Der Tunnel** (1914) expanded the concept into a peaceful vision of a transatlantic tunnel of the future.

Nineteen years later, his book finally reached the screen in German and French versions, both directed by Kurt Bernhardt. **Der Tunnel** (Bavaria Film, 1933) is a much underrated SF film in its German version, a dynamic, realistic portrayal of the perils of constructing a tunnel under the Atlantic. The sets have been called "among the most remarkable ever created for a science fiction film...Their realism may be gauged from the fact that during one sequence the film's associate producer, August Lautenbacher, was killed when the tunnel collapsed."

On-screen disasters, including explosions, flooding, and volcanic eruptions, are superbly staged, and the sweat and grime of the workers often gives a documentary quality to the film. Inspirational speeches drive the men on to complete the job at last, and the tunnel is opened for traffic. Paul Hartmann starred in the German version; Jean Gabin in the French.

Two years later, Maurice Elvey remade the film in a British version called **Transatlantic Tunnel** (also called **The Tunnel**) (Gaumont, 1935). Elvey had included a Channel Tunnel in **High Treason** (1929), but this one was much more impressive, with its gleaming miles of track, and futuristic trains. His now-familiar world of 1940 contained TV phones, global television, advanced automobiles, and the Tunnel, bored under the Atlantic with a "giant fifty-foot radium drill." Curt Siodmak did the adaptation, and the film boasted a distinguished cast: Richard Dix, Leslie Banks, Madge Evans, C. Aubrey Smith, Basil Sydney, and, in cameo appearances, Walter Huston and George Arliss as the American President and the British Prime Minister (not Disraeli).

Elvey's version is interesting enough, his world shining and efficient, but the film must take second place to the energetic and realistic version of Bernhardt.

King Kong (RKO, 1933).

Later in 1933, as if to make up for the disappointment of its earlier release of **Deluge**, RKO proceeded to give the world a hairy blockbuster of a film—**King Kong**! Whether classified as SF, horror, or fantasy, this picture has become a true classic of motion picture history—a masterpiece of imagination and a triumph of technique.

Produced and directed by Merian C. Cooper and Ernest B. Schoedsack from a story by Edgar Wallace and Cooper, the film boasted a stirring and powerful score by Max Steiner, and a technical staff headed by Willis O'Brien of **The Lost World**. His presentation of Kong and the dinosaurs of Skull Island has never been surpassed; and the masterful integration of the many special effects techniques used in the production made **Kong** the most cohesive film ever to combine stop-motion animation with live action process shots.

The story concerns an ambitious film producer named Carl Denham (Robert Armstrong),

(left)   *King Kong* meets Ann Darrow (Fay Wray) amidst the steamy jungles of Skull Island (RKO, 1933).

(above)   Carl Denham (Robert Armstrong) bandages the hand of *Son of Kong* (RKO, 1933).

who wants to give the world a new kind of thriller movie. He assembles a tough crew, hires a destitute ex-actress named Ann Darrow (Fay Wray) for his heroine, and sails for an uncharted island in the South Seas. There are rumors of strange animals on the island, but nobody realizes just how strange! During the voyage, one of the crewmen, John Driscoll (Bruce Cabot), falls in love with Ann.

Arriving at Skull Island, the party discovers a tribe of black savages who have never seen white people before, and they kidnap Ann as a sacrifice to their god Kong, who is kept at bay behind a gigantic wall.

The transmutation machine from *Gold* (*L'Or*) (Ufa, 1934).

Kong, a 50-foot-high monster ape, comes crashing through the trees to claim his offering, and he takes the terrified Ann back to his rocky lair. On the way, they encounter a tyrannosaur, one of the many types of prehistoric animals still alive on the island, and a tremendous battle ensues. Meanwhile, Driscoll and the crew follow the trail to rescue the screaming Ann, battling their own way through a nightmare of carnivorous dinosaurs (including an unjustly-maligned, man-eating brontosaurus: the real things were vegetarians). Several of the crew are killed, and all the rest except Driscoll die at the hands of Kong himself, who has also dispatched the tyrannosaur. But Driscoll persists, and eventually rescues Ann from the giant ape while the primate is distracted by a marauding pterodactyl.

Furious at the loss of his little playmate, whom he has treated with sincere, if rough, affection, Kong comes roaring back to the native village, bursting through the giant gates, and scattering huts and natives like ten-pins. Finally, Kong is subdued by gas bombs, and Denham takes him back to New York in chains to exhibit him as "The Eighth Wonder of the World."

By now the audience is quite sympathetic toward Kong, but when he escapes his captors in New York the full ferocity of his nature asserts itself. He proceeds to trash a good part of the city, derailing an elevated train, and finally climbing up Ann's hotel and kidnapping her right through the twelfth-storey window. After this, the only way for Kong is up, and he takes Ann with him on his classic climb to the top of the Empire State Building. There he fights his last great battle, until swarming biplanes gun him down. Gazing ruefully at the huge corpse, Denham sums it up: "It was beauty killed the beast."

The sheer scope and audacity of the film's concept, and the excellence of its execution, have overcome most of the negative criticism of this film. It was enormously popular and made a lot of money for RKO; it has been re-released in theaters and shown on TV probably more than any other SF film, most recently with the restoration of several scenes censored from the original version. There is always a new generation of film-goers to appreciate its wonders.

The success of **King Kong** caused the producers to rush a sequel, **Son of Kong**, to completion the same year, but it suffers greatly by comparison. Produced by Cooper and directed by Schoedsack, the sequel was written by Ruth Rose, who worked on the original adaptation of **King Kong**. Again, there were fine special effects by O'Brien, with models built by Marcel Delgado; Max Steiner wrote the music.

It is unclear whether a bad conscience or greed causes Carl Denham (again played by Armstrong) to return to Skull Island, but he does, along with Helen Mack, Frank Reicher, and Noble Johnson and Victor Wong (for a little racist comic relief). This time, they discover an even more amazing creature—a baby Kong, dressed in a snowy white pelt. He's much more friendly than his Dad was, and a lot cuter—Denham bandages up a sore paw and makes a large friend for life—and death.

After a few battles with the dinosaurs, little Kong saves Denham from a watery doom at the expense of his own life. A volcanic eruption causes the island to sink beneath the sea, but the ape holds Denham up until a ship can rescue him, and then goes down with Skull Island to a watery grave.

Although still a lot of fun, and with fine (though fewer) special effects, the film was played largely for laughs, virtually a parody of **King Kong**. Much of the humor is inane and tedious, and the film is seldom seen today.

The Japanese revived King Kong in two rather awful sequels, **King Kong vs. Godzilla** (1963) and **King Kong Escapes** (1967), and Herman Cohen produced another giant ape film called **Konga** (AIP, 1960), in which a chimpanzee is scientifically enlarged to enormous size, evidently becoming a gorilla as well!

Finally, in 1976 Dino De Laurentiis produced a $20 million remake of the original **King Kong** for Paramount, with no dinosaurs and no stop-motion animation. A giant 40-foot mechanical ape was constructed, but it was so clumsy and unbelievable that it was used for only a few short scenes. The balance of the film's scenes with Kong were played by a giant mechanical hand (which was well done) and Rick Baker in a monkey suit. Baker, although given short shrift in the film's credits, is responsible for the warmth of the character of Kong in this version, one of its few redeeming features. All the ballyhoo over the film made it a boxoffice hit, but most SF fans roundly condemned it for the cynical, artless production it was. A sequel is threatened.

In Germany, Karl Hartl again directed Hans Albers in another SF thriller, **Gold** (Ufa, 1934). Reaching back into SF literature as far as Poe, screenwriter Rolf Vanloo came up with a modernization of the alchemical tradition in which a scientist in an underwater laboratory (extravagantly designed by Otto Hunte) discovers the means to change lead into gold by atomic bombardment. A young physicist attempts to stop him from destroying the world's economy, but the film fails to generate much interest aside from the scenes in the laboratory. The climax, however, with enormous bolts of lightning playing over the huge machine, is truly spectacular, and was later intercut into the final scenes of **The Magnetic Monster** (UA, 1953), between closeups of Richard Carlson. A simultaneous French version, **L'Or**, was directed by Serge de Poligny.

Gold was more expensive and required more shooting time than **Metropolis**; it was the last gasp of the German cinema's exploration of technological fantasy. The combined influences of

Hollywood and Nazism were to turn German cinema away from the direction of Lang, Rippert, and Wiene, but the SF film would live on in America.

Nineteen thirty-six was another good year for SF films in Hollywood, although the features were still being sold as horror pictures. **The Devil Doll** (MGM, 1936) was based on A. Merritt's horror-fantasy novel, **Burn, Witch, Burn!** (1933), and was produced, directed, and co-written by Tod Browning, famous for **Dracula** (Universal, 1931), **Freaks** (MGM, 1932), and **Mark of the Vampire** (MGM, 1935). Garrett Fort, Guy Endore, and Erich von Stroheim also collaborated on the screenplay, and the distinguished cast included Lionel Barrymore, Maureen O'Sullivan, and Henry B. Walthall.

Although primarily a horror film, its concept of a serum that reduces people and animals to doll size was a superbly visual one, and influenced many subsequent films, notably **Dr. Cyclops** (Paramount, 1940), and **The Incredible Shrinking Man** (Universal, 1957). The use of giant props combined with scenes of process photography was first established in this film, and later improved to perfection for the Universal production.

Despite the presence of a leering Lionel Barrymore as the villain, and some effective scenes of tiny killers stalking their victims, the film is not a success, and remains one of Tod Browning's few embarrassments in the horror film field.

A much more successful blend of horror and SF appeared in **The Invisible Ray** (Universal, 1936), produced by Edmund Grainger and directed by Lambert Hillyer. It boasted the talents of the two top horror stars in Hollywood, Boris Karloff and Bela Lugosi, and struck a successful mood of menace somewhere between the terrifying and the technical.

Dr. Janos Rukh (Boris Karloff) has developed a new type of telescope that can turn back time, and view the heavens as they were millions of years ago. He proves that a meteorite containing a new element, "more powerful than radium," landed in Africa many centuries ago. His friend and colleague, Dr. Benet (Bela Lugosi), agrees to organize an expedition and accompany Rukh to the Dark Continent to search for the meteorite. Once there, Rukh proceeds alone into the Mountains of the Moon, where he locates "Radium X" in a volcanic crater.

But he becomes contaminated by the element—his hands and face glow in the dark and his touch means death. Benet develops a temporary antidote to the radioactive horror, but the poison has begun to affect Rukh's brain. Believing that Benet and the others have stolen his discovery by presenting it to the Scientific Congress, Rukh vows revenge. He has harnessed the element in a ray projector where it can either kill with great destructive power or be used to cure. He experiments on his mother (Violet Kemble Cooper), restoring her eyesight, but then he proceeds to kill off, one by one, just by touching them, the members of the expedition. After an unsuccessful attempt to kill his wife (Frances Drake), Rukh succeeds in murdering Dr. Benet, but Rukh's mother ends his reign of terror by destroying her son's supply of antidote. The poison consumes him completely, and he leaps to his death, a flaming mass of radioactivity.

This film introduced Karloff to a role he would play often during his career, that of a sympathetic scientist whose advanced discovery or invention turns him into a menace, a standard concept for many SF films of the atomic age to come. Here, Karloff had the larger and more difficult role, playing Rukh as cold and dispassionate at first, then progressively slipping into madness. Lugosi, for a change, was restrained and warm—an excellent foil for Karloff.

John P. Fulton's special effects were outstanding, especially in the early scenes, depicting the battle of the suns in the Andromeda galaxy, and the coming of the meteorite to earth. The scenes of Rukh discovering Radium X in the volcano were later used in the Bela Lugosi serial, **The Phantom Creeps** (Universal, 1939).

Two scenes from *The Invisible Ray*. (above left) Karloff, as Dr. Janos Rukh, meets Dr. Benet (Bela Lugosi); (left) Boris Karloff demonstrates his ray projector.

While Hollywood was busy producing its hybrid brand of SF film, England stepped forward with a spectacular example of the genre, the film that lends its title to this book. Alexander Korda's London Films production of **Things to Come** (1936) was the most ambitious SF film since **Metropolis** and the first great sound film in the field.

After years of disappointments, H. G. Wells at last got his chance—in 1934, Korda invited him to do a screen version of his future history book, **The Shape of Things to Come** (1933), and two years later, after four drafts and considerable (acknowledged) assistance from Korda, Lajos Biro, and the director, William Cameron Menzies, it reached the screen.

(preceding pages and below)   Two of the futuristic machines of *Things to Come*, Alexander Korda's epic adaptation of H. G. Wells's scenario. In Wells's future, man becomes involved in a new Thirty Years War, but survives the destruction to build the new Utopia of 2036 A. D. A flawed masterpiece of war and peace.

CF₁
: 226A.

By this time, Wells's literary reputation was so great that many of the people associated with the project felt a bit awed by his presence. He dominated the production to such a degree that he sent out memos regarding even such things as costume and furniture design. He was involved in every stage of the filmmaking.

Korda was apparently afraid to oppose Wells very strongly, and the latter's inexperience in actual cinematic writing is apparent in places where the film bogs down, and becomes too much of a political or philosophical polemic. To a large degree, both the strengths and weaknesses of the film are directly attributable to Wells.

It was not easy for him to extract an acceptable story line from a book that was not fiction to begin with, but rather a discussion of social and political forces and possibilities. However, he did come up with two characters who, although lacking depth dimension, functioned admirably as symbols of the clash between the chaotic old world order and the programmed, scientific sanity of the new.

One of the characters was John Cabal, played by Raymond Massey with just the right touch of grim humor and smug self-sufficiency. Cabal and his wife (Sophie Stewart) are citizens of Everytown in 1940. Together with a friend, Pippa Passworthy (Edward Chapman), they are celebrating Christmas Eve, when the announcement of World War II is heard over the radio. Pass-

John Cabal (Raymond Massey) confronts the Boss (Ralph Richardson) of Everytown, in *Things to Come* (London Films, 1936).

worthy, symbolic of those who never really believed war would come, is shocked, but the more far-seeing Cabal is not surprised.

Shortly after, an air raid is sounded and the town is bombed by massed aircraft that drone ominously overhead, but are never seen. Everytown is demolished, and the film becomes a lengthy montage of fighting and devastation, as the war stretches on and on, driving the world back to barbarism.

Cabal survives and is seen again in a brief vignette as an aviator who shoots down an (obviously German) fighter pilot (John Clements), then tries to save his life. But this is not World War I, and there is no longer any room for "glory and gallantry"—the technological horrors of war win out, and the enemy flier dies from his own poison gas after giving his gas mask to a nearby child. Clearly, Wells was not totally anti-German in his feelings at this time—he still embraced the concept of individual soldiers as ordinary human beings, unwillingly manipulated by their governments. This was not to be a popular sentiment during the forthcoming holocaust, whose advent he predicted so accurately.

The war drags on—futuristic tanks creep over a blasted landscape; a dead soldier, crucified on barbed wire, dissolves into wisps of cloth. Finally, in 1966 general hostilities grind to a halt from lack of resources, and a terrible new plague, the "wandering sickness," terrorizes the survivors.

The only way to deal with the plague-carrying zombies that result from the disease is to shoot them, a drastic but effective solution instigated by a man (Ralph Richardson) who rapidly rises to power as the Boss of the ruined shell of Everytown.

By 1970, the plague has been conquered, the city has begun to rebuild, and the Boss is in full control. Richardson is a blustering, swaggering warlord, determined to carry on hostilities in his own petty domain as long as anyone is left to oppose him. Dressed in a tin helmet with black plumes and moth-eaten furs over a military uniform, the Boss, with his "flags and his follies," is a superb symbol of Wells's pet hates—militarism, politics, and capitalism. The Boss's mistress, Roxana (Margaretta Scott), is barbarically attired with necklaces of coins.

Into this warlike atmosphere comes John Cabal in a sleek, futuristic plane—a striking contrast to the pathetic old crates the Boss has been attempting to activate for his war against the Hill Tribes. He tells the Boss that he is an Airman, one of a group of scientists and technologists in Basra who have banded together to preserve and rebuild civilization. The Boss, seeing Cabal as a threat, but not wanting to admit it, tries to force him to fix up the tattered "air force." "I want those planes!" he bellows unreasonably. When Cabal refuses, he is imprisoned until the Boss's chief engineer, Richard Gordon (Derrick de Marney), craftily asks for Cabal's help in repairing the planes. Gordon hates the Boss, and wants to escape, and with Cabal's assistance he gets one of the ancient biplanes up and flies to Basra.

The Boss has talked himself into believing that Cabal is not really a serious threat to his power, merely some sort of "aerial bus driver"; he is totally unprepared for the massive air strike by the gigantic futuristic bombers of the Airmen, as they come roaring out of the clouds, dropping "peace gas" bombs. The Boss's soldiers are only immobilized, but the Boss himself dies—probably of frustration. He is a dinosaur whose time is past.

Cabal leads the Airmen forward to "a new life for mankind": a montage of futuristic men and machines work together to construct the city of tomorrow, a gleaming, antiseptic utopia embodying all of Wells's hopes and dreams for the future—the beneficient use of science and technology for the happiness and advancement of mankind.

The narrative resumes in the rebuilt Everytown of 2036: a trip to the Moon is planned by

One of Zolok's giant black zombies, from *The Lost City* (Regal, 1935).

Oswald Cabal (also played by Massey), grandson of John Cabal and overseer of the community. But there is a snake in Eden: Theotocopulos (Cedric Hardwicke), a master sculptor, opposes scientific progress. He attempts to lead a mob against the firing of the Space Gun, but to no avail—the first space capsule is fired to the Moon, and reason prevails over emotion. Mankind has taken a giant step forward toward the stars.

As prophecy, **Things to Come** is not remarkable, except for the accuracy of its war prediction, but even then the real thing mercifully lasted for a much shorter duration than predicted. Like many thinkers of his day, Wells feared that a new war would presage the end of western civilization and the onset of a new Dark Age. He tried mightily to warn mankind, and point the way to peace and prosperity as he envisioned it—but few listened. He could see what they would not.

Audiences responded to the visual extravagance of **Things to Come**, but didn't seem to get the message. Korda spent 350,000 pounds to make the film, probably the most ambitious project ever undertaken by a British film unit, but it was a financial failure—only in retrospect can we see it as a flawed but brilliant milestone in the history of the SF film.

The keynote that sets the film apart and gives it its deserved reputation as a classic is the scope of its imagination. For its day, it was bold and unique, its 100-year sweep into the future a daring filmic concept. Cameron Menzies, directing actors for the first time, contributed an impressive and consistent visualization of Wells's future; he and his art director, Victor Korda, working closely with special effects expert Ned Mann, produced a future society with the capricious charm of the newly popular comic strip **Flash Gordon**, but with a sophistication that marks it as very definitely a British film.

Mann's special effects are uneven in places, and often suffer by comparison with those in **Metropolis**, which Wells hated; but such scenes as the emergence of the giant "flying wings" out of the clouds over Everytown, the approach to the Space Gun in the tiny helicopter, and the mob storming the launch site as the preparations to fire the rocket are under way, are unforgettable. And the montage of building the city of tomorrow, with its ingeniously-designed rock blasters, spinning dynamos, and construction machines, is an SF film fan's dream come true.

One of the most significant aspects of **Things to Come** is its musical score, by the eminent British composer, Arthur Bliss. Not only is it an exciting symphonic piece in its own right, but its composition drew the attention of filmmakers, composers, and the public to the importance of the composer's contribution to filmmaking. Bliss was brought in on the production at the beginning and was able to closely interweave music and picture sequences, thereby making the score

Gene Autry, in his first major screen role, fights Queen Tika (Dorothy Christy) and Prime Minister Argo (Wheeler Oakman) in *The Phantom Empire* of Murania (Mascot, 1935).

an element in the film's design. It is interesting, in this era of electronic music and musical effects, to look back and observe how well a traditional—though experimental—symphonic score can work with an advanced cinematic concept.

Bliss, however, felt restricted by the requirements of film composing, and followed the **Things to Come** score with his "Music for Strings," a piece of absolute music, as a kind of "mental purgative." Nevertheless, the score remains one of the best ever composed for a SF picture, and it has become an important part of the history of film music.

Things to Come is at its best when totally visual—its flaws lie in the specious political and social polemics Wells loaded into it. Although they do not really detract from its merit as a film, they are amazingly naive, and even a bit Fascist in light of subsequent realizations in economics and sociology. Technocracy alone is not enough—a dictatorship, even though benign and visionary, like that of Oswald Cabal, is still a dictatorship. The Theotocopuloses of today must have their say as well as the Cabals. Human happiness and well-being require more than Wells's sterile, "whole-wheat-bread utopia" has to offer.

Wells's concept of the Space Gun, borrowed from his predecessor, Jules Verne, was outdated even in the '30s, and he was criticized for its use at the time. His estimate of the 100-year span before a Moon voyage became reality was overly cautious: even he couldn't dream that man would be on the Moon in just over 30 years. His pessimism about the effect of World War II on civilization can now more validly be applied to hypothetical survivors of World War III: the Boss's Everytown, is a very creditable portrait of what a post-atomic society would be like.

But the film transcends Wells's shortcomings, and his vision of man's choice between "all the universe or nothingness" is a fine and inspiring one. Like science fiction visionaries before and after him, Wells sees man's destiny out among the stars. "For man, no rest and no ending. He must go on, conquest beyond conquest. First this little planet with its winds and ways, and then all the laws of mind and matter that restrain him. Then the planets about him, and at last, out across the immensity to the stars. And when he had conquered all the deeps of space and all the mysteries of time, still he will be beginning."

Finally, for better or worse, H. G. Wells had had his say on the screen.

World interest in SF films declined rapidly after 1936. Musicals, gangster films, and horror movies continued to be the public favorites; then, even the horror films began to sink in quality. By the 1940s, except for the work of Val Lewton, certain of Karloff's pictures, and one or two others, the fantastic cinema had declined into grade "Z" quickies, with little to recommend them. SF and horror were almost synonymous terms in audiences' minds, and with good reason.

SF fans were reduced to trivia like **The Gladiator** (Columbia, 1938), a comedy version (with Joe E. Brown) of Philip Wylie's novel of the same name, in which a man is made super-strong by a serum, an idea later utilized in the comic books to create Captain America. The original Wylie novel has also been credited with the inspiration for the more popular comic book hero, Superman. Both he and Captain America later turned up in serials.

Nineteen thirty-nine saw the last gasp of the French SF film, **Le Monde Tremblera (The World Will Shake)** (CICC), directed by Richard Pottier from a screenplay by Henri-Georges Clouzot and J. Villard. It concerned a machine that can predict death, thus causing world-wide disorder, assassinations, and suicides.

It was undistinguished, as was a 1939 British effort, **Q Planes**, released in America as **Clouds Over Europe**. A borderline SF war-scare drama featuring a ray which can halt airplane engines in mid-air, its sole distinction was its cast, which included Laurence Olivier, Valerie Hobson, and Ralph Richardson.

As Wells had predicted, things had rapidly gone from bad to worse in Europe, and Hitler was now ravaging Poland and Czechoslovakia. The war effectively halted film production on the European continent.

During the latter half of the '30s, serials were the only remaining source of SF cinema, as they continued to roll off the studio assembly lines in incredible proliferation. Many of them contained a fine assortment of the traditional SF gadgetry.

The Lost City (Regal, 1935) bombards the viewer with an outrageous and faintly disgusting compendium of SF cliches. William "Stage" Boyd is Zolok, a mad scientist who is devastating the world by reversing the tides, zapping the oceans with a diabolical death ray from his hidden city deep in the African jungle. Kane Richmond goes to investigate, and finds himself in a nightmare of sadism and superscientific marvels masterminded by Zolok, the last survivor of the Ligurians. Zolok has the power to rejuvenate the dead, read thoughts, freeze electricity, turn African natives into giant mindless killing machines—and even turn black men into white.

Today, much of the subject matter of this serial seems distasteful—and even at the time of its release, it was an example of excess seldom encountered on the screen. It has been called

(below)   Two Americans are menaced by the merciless robots of the *Undersea Kingdom* (Republic, 1936).

(right)   Emperor Ming the Merciless (Charles Middleton), from *Flash Gordon* (Universal, 1936).

"the worst serial ever made," but from a technical standpoint, it is remarkably inventive. Perhaps this was due partially to the efforts of SF writer Perley Poore Sheehan, who collaborated on the screenplay.

The serial was banned in Lithuania because of "inhuman treatment," and a two-part comic book adaption appeared in **Giant Comics** and **Choice Comics** in 1942, a rarity in the years before comic book film adaptions became common. A cut-down version was released theatrically as **City of Lost Men.**

The Phantom Empire (Mascot, 1935) was a vehicle for singing cowboy Gene Autry. This 12-chapter cliffhanger launched his career, and started him on the road to incredible popularity.

Autry plays himself, a rancher who operates a radio station on his Texas spread, and is hassled by crooks because his land contains rich deposits of radium. While chasing them, Autry discovers a shaft in a deserted mine leading down to the unknown land of Murania, 20,000 feet below. The Phantom Empire is a strange city of transparent lift tubes, lumbering cardboard robots, and, of course, the ever-present death ray. This cross between **Metropolis** and **Things to Come** is ruled by the wicked Queen Tika (Dorothy Christy), and her prime minister, Argo (Wheeler Oakman), who want to use the robots and the ray to rule the surface world.

Autry is captured by the Muranians; his sidekicks, Frankie Darro, Betsy King Ross, and Oscar (Smiley Burnette), follow him below and are also captured. But they all escape to the surface when a revolt breaks out. The death ray is loosed on the rebels, but goes out of control, and destroys the entire underground kingdom.

This idea was repeated as the climax of George Pal's MGM feature, **Atlantis, the Lost Continent** (1961), a film that is really a serial in disguise.

The Phantom Empire was strangely more effective as SF than anyone had a right to expect. Perhaps this was due to the expert and fast-paced direction of Otto Brower and B. Reeves Eason, or perhaps it comes from the odd juxtaposition of two conflicting film genres, science fiction and the Western.

Whatever the reason, its success spurred Hollywood serial-makers to repeat the formula with **Undersea Kingdom** (Republic, 1936), also co-directed by B. Reeves Eason. The plot was roughly the same. Ray "Crash" Corrigan (playing himself) accompanies a scientist (C. Montague Shaw) on a rocket submarine voyage to the bottom of the ocean, where they discover the lost city of Atlantis under a huge dome.

Hoping to counteract the massive earthquakes that are ravaging the U. S., Crash and the professor discover that the Atlanteans are causing them, under the direction of the villainous Unga Khan (Monte Blue). The inevitable death ray is much in evidence, and the filmmakers outdid themselves in loading this serial with ray guns, an army of robots, an atomic disintegration machine, reflectoplate televisors, rocket planes, and other gadgets. After battles galore (and 12 chapters later), Crash manages to save the surface world from an Atlantean invasion.

But by far the best and most famous of the '30s SF serials are **Flash Gordon** (Universal, 1936) and its two sequels. They possess a vitality and style that sets them apart from all other SF serials, and their popularity remains so great that even today they are often seen on TV.

Larry "Buster" Crabbe was perfectly cast as the golden-haired Flash, hero of the popular 1934 Alex Raymond comic strip. His adversary, the evil Ming the Merciless, was portrayed with great visual exactness by Charles Middleton, but his Midwestern twang was a bit disconcerting. Frank Shannon was a more disheveled Dr. Zarkov than his pen-and-ink counterpart, and Dale Arden's (Jean Rogers) hair was the wrong color. Otherwise, there was as much fantastic action as anyone could ask for, ably directed by Frederick Stephani.

70

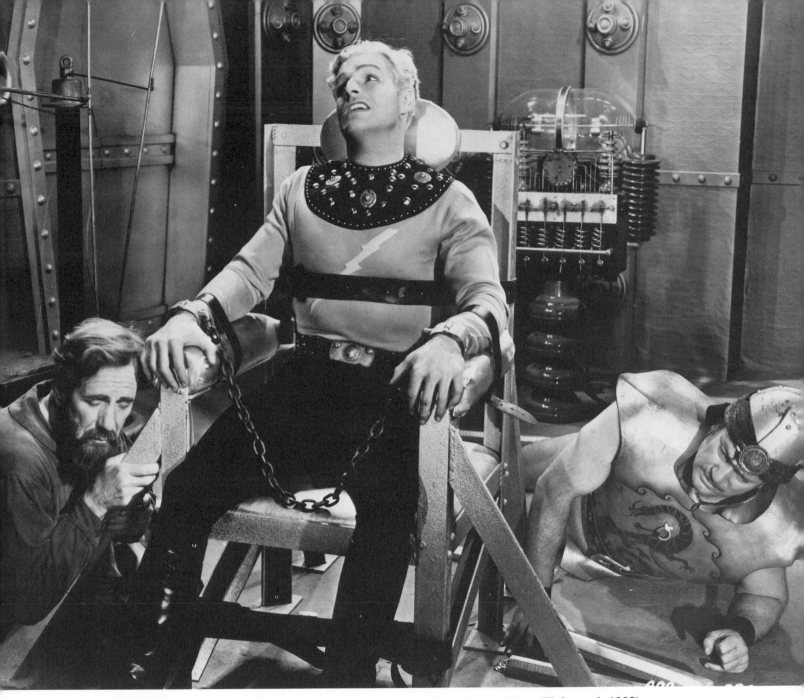

Flash (Buster Crabbe) suffers for mankind in *Flash Gordon's Trip to Mars* (Universal, 1938).

In the first serial, the most expensive ever made ($500,000), Universal pulled out all the stops. The plot followed the comic strip up to a point, then went off on its own through 13 exciting chapters filled with rocket ships, ray guns, floating cities, hawkmen, lionmen, sharkmen, fire dragons, atom furnaces, and assorted monsters, including octosacs, orangopoids, tigrons, and the Gocko.

Audiences were awed by the wonders of the planet Mongo, and by Flash's epic battle with Ming and his minions to save the Earth from destruction by the onrushing planet. Fearless, virile, and ever faithful to his perpetual fiancee Dale, Flash is Siegfried incarnate, a 20th century epic hero battling the forces of evil.

The second serial, **Flash Gordon's Trip to Mars** (Universal, 1938), was directed by Ford Beebee and Robert F. Hill, and does not match the production values and energy of the original.

Flash, Dale, and Zarkov blast off for Mars to locate the source of a mysterious ray that is sucking all the nitrogen from the Earth's atmosphere, causing massive earthquakes and cyclones.

The ray is linked to a device planted on Earth by two giant Martians, now dead.

Landing on Mars, Flash and his friends are captured by the Clay Men, who want them to steal the White Sapphire of the evil Queen of Magic, Azura (Beatrice Roberts): the sapphire is the source of her power over the Clay Men. Azura allies herself with a visiting Ming, on loan from Mongo, whose great "Nitrogen Lamp" is destroying the Earth; he is also fomenting war between the Clay Men and the Tree Men in order to gain control of Mars. Flash destroys Azura's sapphire and Ming's ray lamp, and the evil "Emperor of the Universe" perishes in a Disintegration Chamber. **Flash Gordon** made millions for Universal, and earned Buster Crabbe the title "King of the Sound Serials." The sequel was originally called **Flash Gordon and the Witch Queen of Mongo**, the title of a Big Little Book version of the newspaper story. But in October, 1938, Orson Welles broadcast his famous radio version of H. G. Wells's **The War of the Worlds** and scared half the country out of its wits. Mars was on everybody's lips, so the studio quickly changed the locale of the serial from Mongo to Mars and the title to match.

Flash's final appearance was in **Flash Gordon Conquers the Universe** (Universal, 1940), directed by Ford Beebee and Ray Taylor, and loosely based on the Big Little Book, **Flash Gordon and the Ice World of Mongo**. Although not up to the standards of the first two serials, this one boasted handsome and stylish costuming, and interesting set designs.

A deadly epidemic, "The Plague of the Purple Death," threatens earth, as Flash, Dale (now played by Carol Hughes), and Zarkov go rocketing off into space once again. A miraculously unharmed Ming is spreading the plague, but Flash and Zarkov manage to stop him after 12 chapters. He is finally killed for sure and his city destroyed.

All three serials have been cut down and released as feature films for theatrical and TV showings under many different titles. Also an amusing, X-rated parody called **Flesh Gordon** (Graffiti) was released in 1974.

One other SF serial was made starring Buster Crabbe, this time playing the other great SF comic strip hero, **Buck Rogers** (Universal, 1939). Ford Beebee and Saul A. Goodkind directed. Based loosely on the 1928 and 1929 novels by Phillip Francis Nowlan, **Armageddon—2419 A. D.** and **The Airlords of Han**, and the 1929 comic strip they inspired, the story of Buck's fight against tyranny and evil in the 25th century was highly topical to audiences in 1939.

Buck and his pal Buddy Wade (Jackie Moran) sleep for 500 years when their dirigible, carrying a new gas called "Nirvano," crashes on a mountain top. They awake to find the world controlled by the evil Killer Kane (Anthony Warde).

Taken to the Hidden City, they meet Dr. Huer (C. Montague Shaw) and Wilma Deering (Constance Moore), who enlist Buck and Buddy in the fight against Kane. Buck, Wilma, and Buddy rocket to Saturn to gain support in their battle, but Kane's men follow and capture them, managing to talk the oriental Saturnians into helping Kane instead.

But the trio later quell a rebellion of the sub-human Zuggs, and earn the gratitude of the Saturnian leader, Prince Tallen (Phillip Ahn), who then agrees to help them. With the cooperation of the Saturnians, Buck launches an attack on Kane's stronghold and defeats him.

Although little more than a pale imitation of the Flash Gordon serials, **Buck Rogers** does have its share of thrills and plenty of action, and SF fans were ecstatic over all the SF gadgetry transferred to the screen: ray guns, anti-gravity belts, invisible rays, rocket ships, and mind-controlling helmets.

Dr. Alexander Thorkel (Albert Dekker) searches for his miniaturized guinea pigs, in *Dr. Cyclops* (Paramount, 1940).

This serial was also edited and released in several feature versions: **Planet Outlaws** (1953) and **Destination Saturn** (1965).

Nineteen forty brought yet another "first" to SF film history: the first Technicolor production, **Dr. Cyclops** (Paramount). The color was still not perfect, but it was a long way from the primitive efforts of **The Mysterious Island** (1929).

Once again played primarily for horror effects, **Dr. Cyclops** was directed by Ernest B. Schoedsack of **King Kong** fame from a screenplay by Tom Kilpatrick, and carried the ingenious idea of human miniaturization a step beyond its debut in **The Devil Doll** (1936).

Albert Dekker adds a tall, bald-domed, myopic Dr. Alexander Thorkel to the screen's distinguished roster of mad scientists. In his laboratory, located deep in the jungles of Peru near a deposit of radioactive ore, Thorkel is conducting experiments in size reduction. When four scientists and a handyman arrive, Thorkel cannot resist the chance to use them as guinea pigs, and shrinks them all down to doll size.

They escape, but find their suddenly enormous world a terrifying place. They are faced with such horrors as a cat, a chicken, an alligator, a rainstorm that threatens to drown them, and the doctor himself, trying to recapture his Tom Thumb prey.

The little people use all their ingenuity in an attempt to shoot the doctor with his own shotgun,

but fail. Their next plan is aimed at the doctor's coke-bottle glasses, without which he is almost blind. This time they succeed, except for one lens in one pair. The furious doctor rages after them, killing one, but finally trapping himself in a plunge down his radioactive mine shaft. A few days later, the effects of the treatment wear off, and the survivors regain their normal size.

Dr. Cyclops was not a success in 1940, but later exposure on television has shown that it is a much better than average example of the SF-horror film. Albert Dekker is properly cold and sadistic, tormenting his tiny victims as a cat plays with a mouse; the special effects are considerably advanced beyond those in **The Devil Doll**; and the parallel between the Cyclops in the **Odyssey** and the one-eyed Thorkel is well handled. **Dr. Cyclops** remains the only really outstanding SF film produced during the 1940s, as the more realistic horrors of war replaced the cinematic thrills of Hollywood filmmakers. The movie was novelized later that same year by top SF writer Henry Kuttner under the pen-name ''Will Garth.''

Another ambitious but misguided effort of 1940 was **One Million B. C.**, produced and directed by Hal Roach. Reaching way back into SF film history to D. W. Griffith's **Man's Genesis** (1912) and **Brute Force** (1913), Roach concocted a new version of man's prehistory. Reportedly, the aging Griffith himself was hired as associate producer.

Without a budget for model animation, the film made do with process shots of lizards, baby alligators, and iguanas, a pathetically inadequate substitution for stop-motion dinosaurs.

Victor Mature, Carole Landis, and Lon Chaney Jr. tried to lend some dignity to their grunting dialogue, but the whole production was inept, and at times openly ludicrous.

Curt Siodmak, now safely ensconced in Hollywood along with many of his fellow German filmmakers, published a novel in 1943 called **Donovan's Brain**, which has become a kind of minor classic. In 1944, it was made into a low-budget horror film called **The Lady and the Monster** (Republic), starring Vera Ralston, Richard Arlen, and Erich von Stroheim.

This gruesome but implausible story of a human brain kept alive after its owner's body has died, exerting telepathic control over the minds of others, strained mightily to be better than it was, but failed. It was too slow-paced and cluttered with banal theatrics. Professor von Stroheim was the very embodiment of Nazi atrocities when he uttered lines like, ''When you are trying to solve the mysteries of nature, it doesn't matter whether you experiment with humans or guinea

(left) The dinosaurs attack, in *One Million B.C.* (United Artists, 1940).

(right) The great ape from RKO's 1949 film, *Mighty Joe Young*, a later version of *King Kong*.

pigs." No wonder he was awarded the title, "The Man You Love to Hate."

As the war dragged on, SF film fans were reduced to pathetic attempts like **White Pongo** (PRC, 1945), about a white gorilla of high intelligence, supposedly a missing link. Unknowingly, this creature was the prototype of Bigfoot and the "Abominable Snowman," later to appear in schlock films of the '50s and '60s.

Nineteen forty-five brought the atomic bomb and the end of the war. It also brought SF up to date with a very big bang—the weapon that had been predicted for so long by so many SF writers, from H. G. Wells to Phil Nowlan, was now a reality. After the war, there was an increased public interest in SF literature, and eventually, lagging behind as always, in SF films. It was to be five years before the bright new cycle of SF films would arrive. In them, we were to find the perfect visual expression of the world's growing atomic paranoia.

Meanwhile, SF film fans had nothing on the horizon except **Unknown Island** (Film Classics, 1948), an atrocious update of the **Lost World** idea. It includes belligerent tyrannosaurs (men in dinosaur suits) and an orange ape that attempts to pass itself off as a giant sloth. An abomination.

The last SF picture of any significance in the Forties was **Mighty Joe Young** (RKO, 1949). The old **King Kong** team was back in action, and the result was a new version of the same old story, but with a certain charm and humor, and even tinted sequences!

Merian C. Cooper produced, Ernest B. Schoedsack directed, Ruth Rose did the screenplay, and best of all, Willis O'Brien and Marcel Delgado returned to handle the special effects. Among the members of O'Brien's team this time was a newcomer named Ray Harryhausen, who would go on to become the master's most distinguished pupil. O'Brien finally won a much-deserved Oscar for this film, but on the whole, the model work was not up to his usual standard. Joe's relative size seems to change from scene to scene even more noticeably than Kong's did. At times, Joe seems little larger than the people around him, while other scenes make him appear huge.

But the sequence in which Joe is displayed in the Golden Safari, a nightclub, which he demolishes in an incredible tour de force of special effects destruction, is truly worthy of the man who made **King Kong.**

Robert Armstrong returns to lead an expedition to Africa to capture a giant gorilla, the pet of Terry Moore. He tries to have his troop of cowboys lasso Joe, but the ape fights them off. Armstrong then succeeds in selling Terry the old "glamor of show-biz" routine, and persuades her to take Joe back to America to appear as a nightclub sensation.

Joe puts up with the humiliation of holding Terry and a grand piano aloft while she plays "Beautiful Dreamer," engaging in a tug-of-war with 12 wrestlers, and capering for large paper coins dressed as an organ grinder's monkey. But enough is enough, and an enraged Joe finally proceeds to take the joint apart, releasing caged wild animals who are part of the decor.

After this orgy of violence, Joe flees; but he's a much nicer chap than his cousin Kong was, and he feels ashamed of himself.

To make amends, Joe becomes a hero by rescuing children from a burning orphanage in the film's rousing climax. Then he and Terry return happily to Africa—they have had enough of "civilization."

Thus ended two decades which had seen a depression, a world war, and the atomic bomb. The stage was set for the SF film's adolescence—a time that began with bright promise, but soon degenerated into crippling disappointment, as the SF films of the 1950s retreated from imaginative story lines and concepts into the bottomless mire of cheap horror and shock values. But movies like **King Kong** had pointed the way. Just around the corner were greater things to come.

MONSTERS AND
MENACES
(1950–1959)

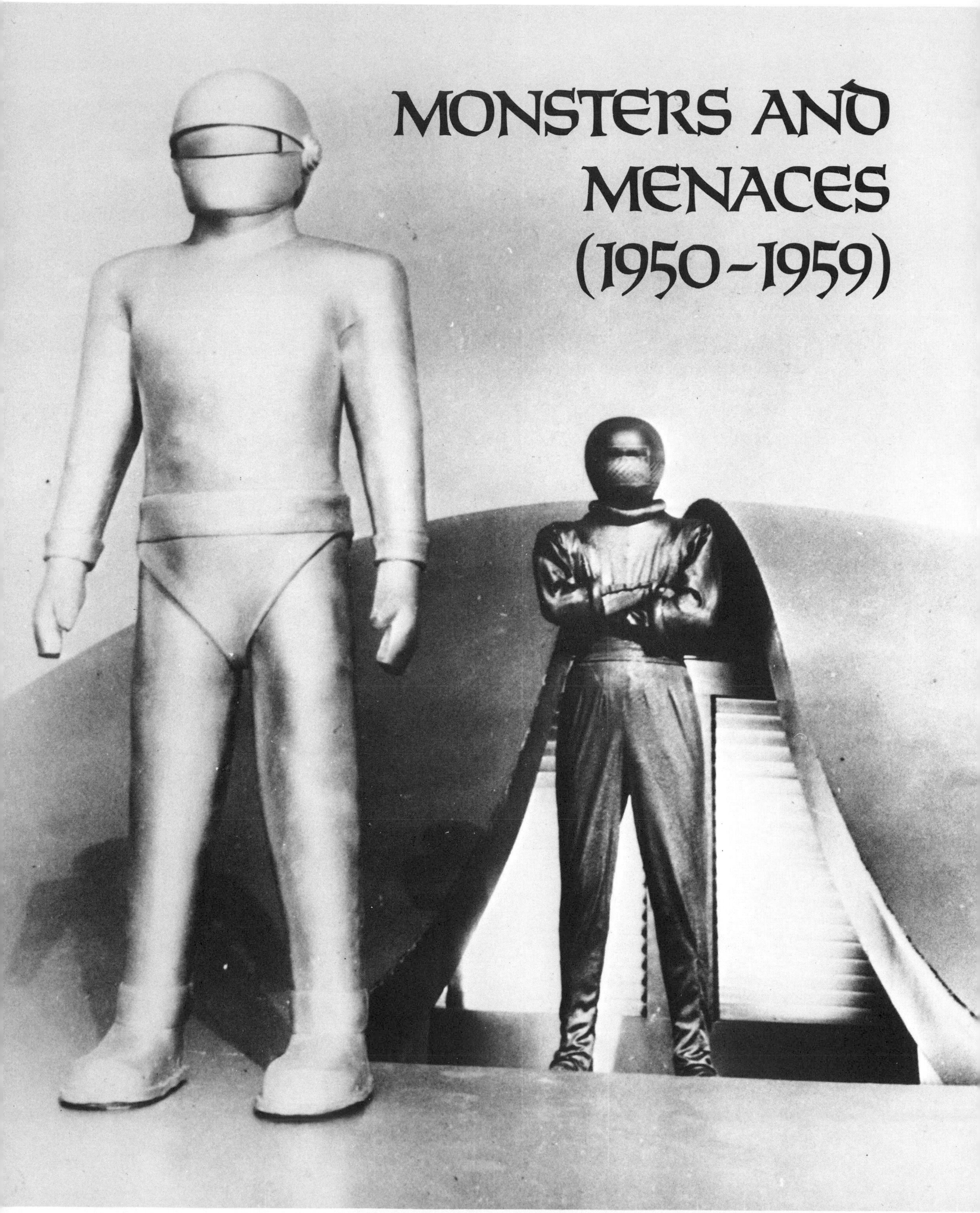

Although the Fifties produced a great many science fiction films, most were lamentable for their low production standards, poor scripts, wretched acting, and cheap special effects. The first two SF films of the decade, **Rocketship X-M** and **Destination Moon**, were enormous commercial successes, and soon had spawned dozens of imitators, ranging from a handful of sensitive and intelligent treatments of science fiction themes, to a great number of mediocre exploitation films that are barely watchable by today's standards, to an unfortunately large number of trashy rip-offs that included some of the worst pictures ever put on film.

By the middle of the decade, the number of monster and creature-from-outer space films threatened to choke out entirely all serious SF productions. Fortunately, even during the height of this period, from about 1954-1958, there were still a few motion picture directors who managed to break lose from the stereotyped creations of their competitors, producing such interesting pictures as **Forbidden Planet, Invasion of the Body Snatchers,** and **1984**.

Floyd Oldham (Lloyd Bridges), Lisa Van Horn (Osa Massen), Karl Eckstrom (John Emery), and Harry Chamberlain (Hugh O'Brien), four of the intrepid astronauts of *Rocketship X-M*, are confronted by the strange inhabitants of Mars.

A *Flying Disc Man from Mars*, from the serial of the
same name (Republic, 1951).

The generally low level of science fiction films in the middle and late 1950s paralleled a similar phenomenon in science fiction literature. The founding of **The Magazine of Fantasy and Science Fiction** in 1949, and **Galaxy Magazine** in 1950, and the simultaneous establishment of specialty book publishers, sparked a renewed interest in the field. Suddenly, there was money to be made in science fiction, and hundreds of publishers jumped into the field. At one point, nearly a hundred magazines were being published. Several paperback companies started SF lines, and Doubleday decided to produce its own hardcover series. Interestingly, the launching of Sputnik in late 1957 seemed to burst the bubble; by 1958, sales of science fiction books and magazines were plummeting, and only a few of the quality publications managed to survive. Similarily, the monster and exploitation films had started to decline in number by 1959; but the production of **On the Beach** and **Journey to the Center of the Earth** later that year promised significantly greater things to come.

Rocketship X-M (Lippert, 1950) was intended to cash in on the massive publicity and popularity of **Destination Moon** (see below). After hearing about George Pal's plans for his science fiction epic, Kurt Newmann (Producer, Director, and Screenwriter) rushed through his own project, beating Pal's film by a few weeks. Five astronauts, Floyd Oldham (Lloyd Bridges), Lisa Van Horn (Osa Massen), Karl Eckstrom (John Emery), William Corrigan (Noah Beery, Jr.), and Harry Chamberlin (Hugh O'Brien), blast off to the Moon. Diverted by a meteor shower, the craft heads for a crash-landing on Mars. Mars has been devastated in some earlier era by an atomic war; only ruins remain, inhabited by a few debased, half-clothed survivors who have reverted to barbarism. The Martians capture the astronauts soon after their landing. But several of the spacemen escape, and blast off for Earth. However, the spaceship was never meant to take them such distances, and their fuel runs out. After warning Earth of the perils of nuclear brinksmanship, Rocketship X-M crashes to Earth, killing everyone aboard.

Like most science fiction pictures of its time, **Rocketship X-M** was filmed on a shoe string, and features technological apparatus that now appear outdated. But the story still retains some power as a parable on the destructive potentials of nuclear energy; its low-key ending is an interesting switch on the man-shall-triumph-over-monster-and-machine denouement so common during this period.

George Pal's **Destination Moon** (Eagle-Lion, 1950), adapted from Robert A. Heinlein's novel, **Rocket Ship Galileo,** was a serious attempt to forecast man's first trip to the Moon. When the U. S. government fails to support an atomic-powered rocket engine developed by Dr. Carsgraves (Warner Anderson), the scientist takes his invention to Jim Barnes (John Archer), a wealthy industrialist. Barnes recognizes the potential of outer space, and the political significance of having the first manned rocket in orbit; he therefore agrees to finance the project, thwarting a Russian effort to get into space first. Soon the craft is ready, and Barnes, Carsgraves, General Thayer (Tom Powers), and Joe Sweeny (Dick Wesson) are on their way to the Moon. The astronauts land, perform the usual scientific experiments, and then discover that they have miscalculated the fuel needed to return. After stripping the ship bare, they still need another two hundred pounds; Sweeny, the radar man, isolates himself outside in the one remaining suit, volunteering to sacrifice his life so the others can return. At the last moment, Barnes rips out the ship's radio, and saves the day by tossing it out the door, together with Sweeny's suit. The rocket returns to Earth with all its crew intact.

Destination Moon was an immensely popular and successful film from a commercial point of view, and it represented Pal's first excursion into the science fiction and fantasy world. Unfortunately, the movie has been dated very markedly by subsequent events; that private industry

The astronauts of the first manned flight to the Moon begin unloading their experimental equipment, in *Destination Moon* (Eagle-Lion, 1950), adapted from a novel by Robert A. Heinlein.

could have financed the enormous investment needed to take man to the Moon seems, in retrospect, rather shortsighted. The acting is wooden, even for a film where the special effects are the main show. All things considered, **Moon** is less interesting as cinema than a picture like **Rocketship X-M**, which is more imaginative; its significance lies mainly in its timing, rather than its treatment.

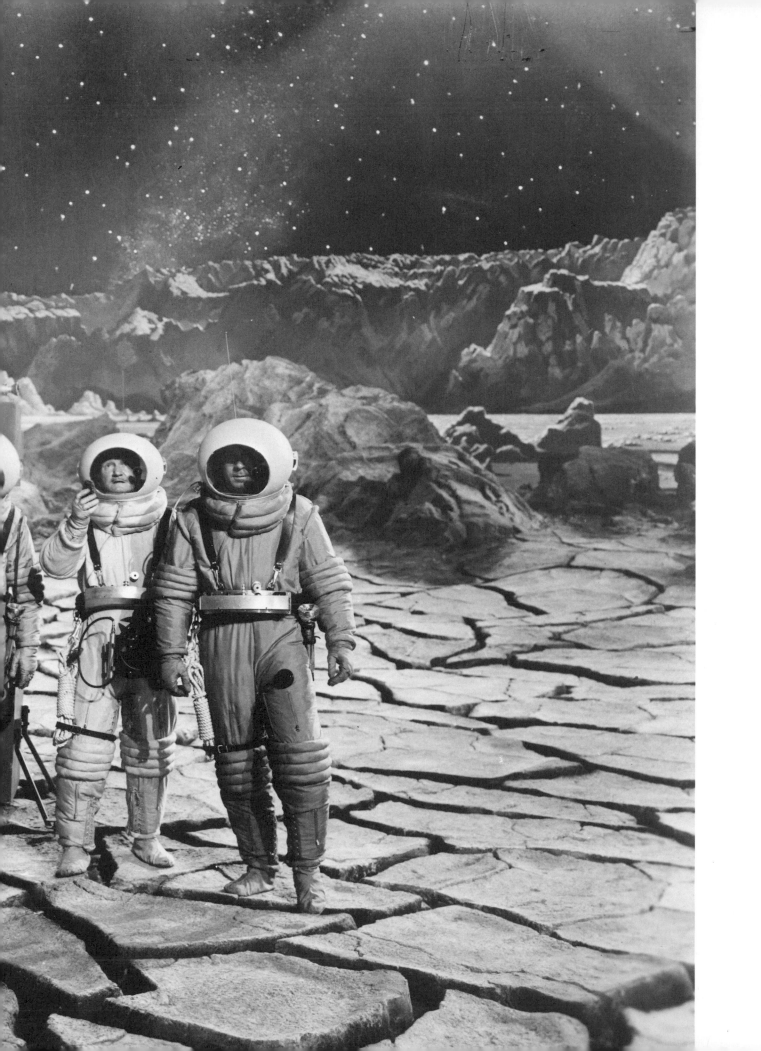

(preceding pages)   The first men on the Moon: Warner Anderson, John Archer, Tom Powers, and Dick Wesson, from *Destination Moon* (Eagle-Lion, 1950).

(below)   The vegetable alien, embedded in a block of ice, perplexes the scientists of a Polar Experimental station, in *The Thing* (RKO, 1951).

Loosely adapted from John W. Campbell's short novel, "Who Goes There?" **The Thing** (RKO, 1951), also called **The Thing from Another World**, is an effective portrayal of man's first meeting with a strange being from outer space. A curious formation in the Arctic wastes draws the attraction of American scientists stationed at an army research station. There, embedded in the ice, is a space ship that obviously could not have been the work of man. Attempts to retrieve the craft result in its destruction; however the ice-encrusted body of the pilot is found nearby, and placed in a shed for future study. The heat of the room thaws out the alien, and it suddenly comes to life.

Immediately, the men are battling for their lives, as the creature (James Arness) strives to get the blood it needs to grow its young. The alien, it seems, is a walking vegetable, an intelligent form of plant life unlike anything evolved on Earth. It can survive the Arctic cold without damage, regenerate limbs at will, and walk through a hail of bullets unharmed. Attempts to communicate with the being are fruitless (either it can't or won't understand), and Captain Hendry (Kenneth Tobey) makes the decision to destroy the creature before it destroys them. Using his men as bait, the army officer lures the alien onto a metal grating, throws the power switch, and "Thing" goes up in smoke.

Despite the possibilities for unintentional comedy, **The Thing** is nicely underplayed, with superior acting and directing. The monster itself is kept in the shadows most of the time, allowing the viewer to imagine the worst for himself. The Arctic setting only heightens the tension, as man

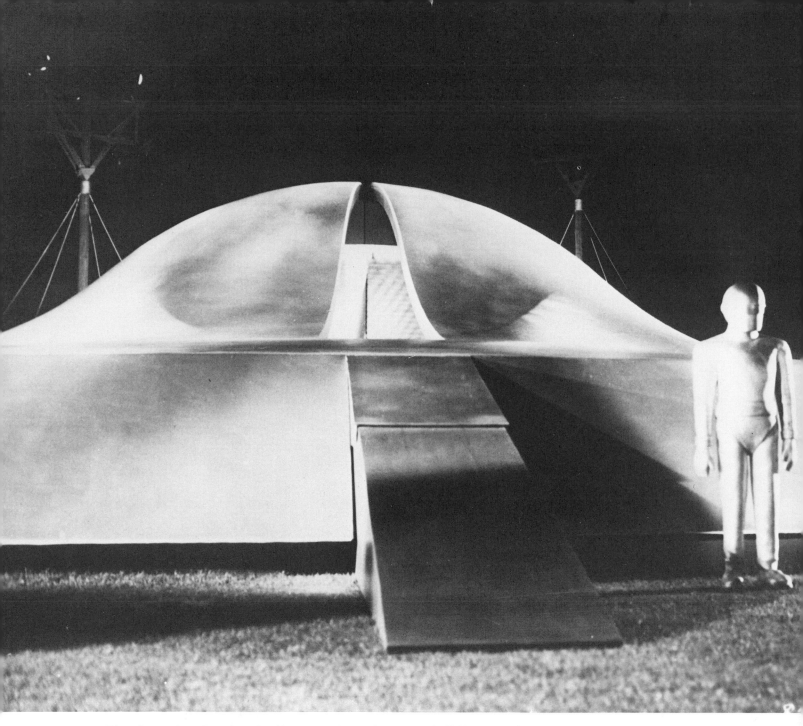

The giant robot Gort stands silent guard over its master's flying saucer, in *The Day the Earth Stood Still* (Twentieth Century-Fox, 1951).

must fight alien and inhospitable climate alike. Much of the credit for the film's effectiveness must go to Producer Howard Hawks, who assisted Director Christian Nyby behind the scenes. The success of **The Thing** (it had several different releases) spurred the movie-makers into producing a myriad of cheap imitations, featuring every imaginable creature the make-up artists could conjure up. Few came anywhere near the quality of the original.

In **The Day the Earth Stood Still** (Twentieth Century-Fox, 1951), based on the story "Farewell to the Master," by Harry Bates, the aliens come to Earth as friends of mankind. A huge flying saucer unexpectedly lands in a Washington, D. C., park, disgorging an eight-foot high robot named Gort, and a mild-mannered, silver-suited human called Klaatu. The army surrounds the craft, and as Klaatu (Michael Rennie) comes forward with his gift for the American president, the soldiers shoot the alien without waiting for him to speak. Klaatu is taken to the local hospital, where he is placed under close guard. Rennie demands to meet with the rulers of Earth, and when his request is denied, escapes from his captors, seeking out Dr. Barnhardt (Sam Jaffe).

He tells Barnhardt that unless the scientists of Earth convene to hear his message, the world will be destroyed. As a demonstration of his power, he completely shuts down the world's electricity (except hospitals and other emergency facilities) for a half hour. Meanwhile, the FBI is still trying to locate the alien, whom they now regard as an imposter. Klaatu has made friends with Helen Benson (Patricia Neal), and is forced to flee with her when government agents begin closing in. He tells her that if he is killed, the robot will begin raging out of control, unless she goes to it, and repeats a certain formula. Shortly thereafter, Rennie is shot down in cold blood, and his body is placed in a jail cell.

Klaatu (Michael Rennie) shows Helen Benson (Patricia Neal) his space craft, with Gort standing by—*The Day the Earth Stood Still* (Twentieth Century-Fox, 1951).

Gort suddenly awakens from his statuesque pose, his controlling factor gone; but Helen confronts the giant metal visage of the automaton, repeating Rennie's words. The robot hesitates, and then lumbers off through the city, where he retrieves the body of his master, and brings it back to the saucer. Helen follows the robot in through the automatic door. Klaatu's body is placed in a special alcove, and his life restored, temporarily, through the marvels of other-worldly science. In a moving finale, as the scientists begin filling the chairs hastily erected in front of the saucer, suddenly the ramp extends itself, and the newly-risen alien strides out, his face set and grim. His people fear mankind's rampant aggressiveness, he says, and the planetary federation which he represents has decreed that atomic weapons must be abolished, and all wars must cease, or Earth will be destroyed by the giant robot he is leaving behind. He returns to the saucer, and the ship takes off.

Director Robert Wise intelligently decided to illustrate his message with a minimum of pyrotechnics. Rennie comes across as a quiet, sensitive, very human being, whose mental and moral superiority to the governmental bureaucrats and army generals is evident from the first scenes. It's only when he mixes with the average American citizens that one gets the feeling he's satisfied with what he sees. In his final confrontation with the Earthmen, Rennie shows us another side, as his strong, firm voice chides the adolescents of Earth, and warns them to correct themselves, or be punished by their superiors. Man must earn his right to the stars; it will not be handed to him. And if he fails to shape up, his incorrigibility will be punished in the only way possible, through his extermination. **The Day the Earth Stood Still** has taken an old science fiction theme, and given it new life; it stands as one of the best SF films of its decade.

When Worlds Collide (Paramount, 1951), George Pal's second foray into science fiction, was adapted from the novel of the same name by Philip Wylie and Edwin Balmer. David Randall (Richard Derr) becomes acquainted with Dr. Hendron (Larry Keating), who tells him that Earth is destined for destruction when the twin planets Zyra and Bellus finish their swing through the solar system. One of the planets, Zyra, will bypass the Earth, and assume Earth's position in orbit around the Sun; the other world will strike Earth several days later, completely destroying both worlds. Randall persuades billionaire Sydney Stanton (John Hoyt) to finance a rocket ship escape mission for a handful of survivors, in the hope that Zyra will prove habitable, and give man a home where he may thrive again.

Meanwhile, Randall has fallen in love with Joyce Hendron (Barbara Rush), the scientist's daughter. The construction of the craft moves forward at a feverish rate, with the help of several hundred volunteers. The forty passengers will be selected from the workers by lot. As the alien worlds grow nearer, Earth begins feeling the effect of the twin planet's gravitational pull, causing spectacular earthquakes, the flooding of several large cities along the seaboard, and other natural disasters. When the craft is completed, the passengers are chosen, and the others, disappointed at their luck, storm the ship. But Randall blasts off in time, and the spacemen are able to watch the destruction of Earth through their portholes. After a crash landing on Zyra, the children of Earth emerge from their capsule to find fresh, breathable air, and the green, lush signs of a brand new Eden.

The special effects carry the day in this film. Pal's cataclysmic scenes of death and destruction match anything done in cinematic history, including the recent spate of disaster epics. The

(following pages) The destruction of New York City, as (viewing clockwise) the busy streets are suddenly flooded in eight feet of water, overwhelmed by a second surge of the sea, and completely inundated when the oceans leave their beds.—*When Worlds Collide* (Paramount, 1951).

89

The Man from Planet X (United Artists, 1951) featured Robert Clarke as a reporter who thwarts an invasion from outer space by the peculiar denizens a doomed planet.

space ship is rather tinny, but typical of its time, complete with fins and launching ramp. The final end of Earth is suitably impressive. Still a film worth seeing, **When Worlds Collide** is one man's vision of the end of the world, and the birth of another.

Man's tampering with the unfathomable forces of nature produces unexpected results, in **The Beast from 20,000 Fathoms** (Warner Brothers, 1953). A nuclear test in the Arctic releases a gigantic dinosaur from its eons-old prison of ice. After being spotted by Professor Elson (Cecil Kellaway), the rhedosaurus heads south towards New York City harbor, its traditional spawning ground. In the process, of course, much of Manhattan gets trampled by the perplexed beast, who also infects the human population with primitive bacteria. Cornered in an amusement park, the creature is neatly dispatched with a radioactive isotope shot through its scaly hide.

The Beast from 20,000 Fathoms was the first picture to be (very loosely) adapted from a Ray Bradbury story, "The Foghorn." Unfortunately, Bradbury's moving tale of a dinosaur seeking its mate in the sound of a foghorn is somehow lost in the transfer to the screen. This film also marks

The Beast from 20,000 Fathoms (Warner, 1953) menaces the streets of New York.

the solo debut of animator Ray Harryhausen, who had worked on several other films prior to this time, but had never before been given free rein to do as he pleased. Harryhausen went on to create many other bizarre creatures, and is currently regarded as perhaps the finest animator in the business. **Beast** is also noteworthy in being the first of a long string of prehistoric monster films, most of which failed to match the mediocrity of the original. A minor film, but still of interest for its excellent model work.

Beginning with Arch Oboler's **Bwana Devil**, a jungle movie, a new craze swept the motion picture industry, as the 3-D process was introduced to the Screen. Science fiction was not immune, of course, and two 3-D pictures were produced in quick succession. **It Came from Outer Space** (Universal, 1953), was based on an original treatment by Ray Bradbury, although Bradbury did not actually write the screenplay (it was adapted by Harry Essex). A space craft from outer space makes a forced emergency landing in the Arizona desert. The only witness to the landing is John Putnam (Richard Carlson), who sees the huge vehicle burrow its way into the desert soil. Putnam tries to persuade the people of Sand Rock, Arizona, that something strange is going on, but no one will listen, until certain of the townfolk begin turning up with radically altered personalities.

Putnam continues his investigations, and discovers that the aliens are making vital repairs to their damaged spaceship; fearing that their appearance will disturb the primitive humans, they have temporarily assumed the shapes of certain members of that species, so they can obtain the necessary supplies. Putnam is promised by the creatures, who resemble giant blobs with great, looming, single eyes, that the townsmen will be restored to their former characters when the aliens are finished with them. After a brief attempt by the Earthmen to storm the vehicle, and the timely

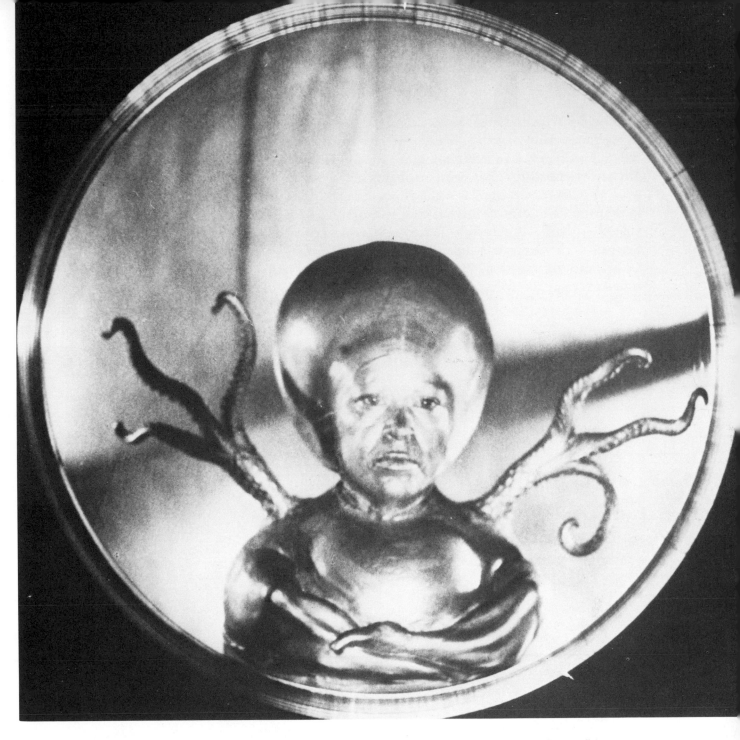

(left)   Ectoplasmic aliens confront John Putnam (Richard Carlson).—*It Came from Outer Space*.

(above)   The controlling brain from *Invaders from Mars* (Twentieth Century-Fox, 1953).

intervention of Putnam between the two forces, the blobs return the humans, and blast off.

Despite the title, **It Came from Outer Space** is a quiet, intelligent plea for tolerance between two dissimilar but intelligent forms of life. Director Jack Arnold deserves credit for avoiding the pervasive paranoia that filled most of the outer space epics filmed during this period. The influence of the aliens is seen through the reaction of their human surrogates; when a townsman makes the mistake of staring up at the Sun without blinking, we recognize that something is seriously wrong. Arnold has made a thoroughly interesting film, one worth seeing again, a picture that deserves its reputation as a minor classic of science fiction cinema.

Another 3-D film was **Invaders from Mars** (Twentieth Century-Fox, 1953), the last film directed by William Cameron Menzies. David MacLean (Jimmy Hunt), a boy of about ten, sees a flying saucer land near his house. He tells his family and friends about the strange events, and they, of course, refuse to believe him. His father (Leif Erickson) is finally prodded to investigate, but he returns with a changed personality and a slight wound on his neck. Other people rapidly become marked with similar signs of possession (the Martians have implanted crystalline devices in their necks to control the humans' mentality). Finally, Dr. Pat Blake (Helena Carter) is convinced by the boy's pleadings, after George MacLean is caught trying to kill one of the remaining normals. The army surrounds the saucer, and invades the sanctuary of the aliens. There are several different versions of the ending: in one, the spaceship escapes; in another, the spaceship is destroyed by the army; in a third, the battle is unresolved. In most existing prints, the film ends

A three-fingered Martian menaces Gene Barry and Ann Robinson, in George Pal's *War of the Worlds* (Paramount, 1953), adapted from the novel by H. G. Wells.

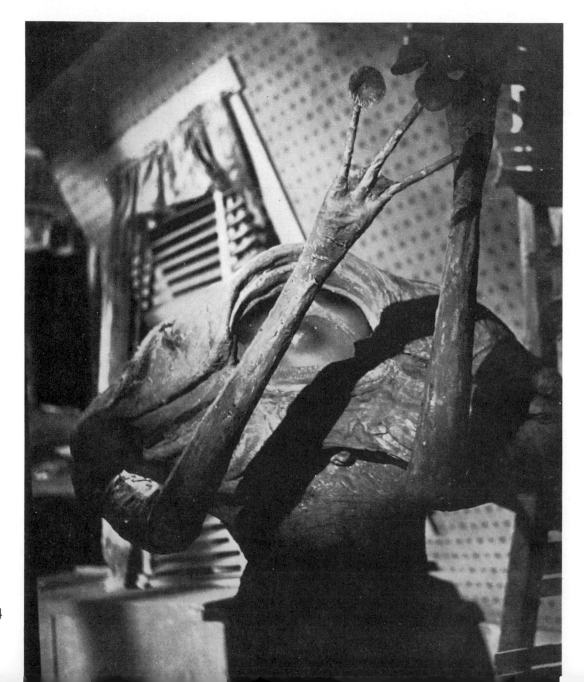

with the boy waking up again in his bedroom, and discovering that it has all been a dream—until he looks outside, and sees the flying saucer landing.

Invaders from Mars was badly mutilated after its initial release, and apparently no true print of the original conception still exists. For this reason, the picture has had very little impact, and has not received the kind of critical attention it deserves. **Invaders** is everyone's nightmare: a world in which no one will listen, where friends become enemies overnight, a world in which the individual must fall back on his own resources to defeat the forces of evil. Menzies questions the very nature of reality: is David's dream real? Or is the second flying saucer just another dream? We never find out for sure.

H. G. Wells's stories have been brought to the screen in many different versions, but **War of the Worlds** was not filmed until George Pal persuaded Paramount to finance the project in 1953. Pal updated Wells's story by changing the setting to Southern California, and making the time frame more contemporary. A meteorite plunges to Earth near a small California town, and the military soon surrounds the pit where the rock is still steaming. Suddenly, a section of the thing unscrews, and out of the suddenly revealed space craft rise several flying machines, topped with snake-like proboscises, and riding on what appear to be anti-gravity beams. The army, clergy, and bystanders are quickly pulverized with heat beams, and the rampage of destruction begins.

Clayton Forrester (Gene Barry), a nuclear physicist, witnesses the initial depredations of the Martians, but escapes with the clergyman's niece, Sylvia Van Buren (Ann Robinson). The pair are cornered in an abandoned farmhouse by a Martian vehicle, where they manage to just glimpse one of the aliens (large, man-sized creatures with bulbous heads, and single eyes in the center of their foreheads), and barely escape its clutches. Meanwhile, the military has not been idle, and is preparing to drop an atomic bomb on the flying machines. But man's best efforts prove futile, and the onslaught continues. Forrester and Van Buren seek refuge in the ruins of Los Angeles, huddling with other survivors in a small church. The sounds of destruction grow ever nearer, and all appears lost, until an unearthly silence drops over the city. The machines have fallen to earth, their creatures struck down by Earthly germs for which they have no immunity.

War of the Worlds remains an interesting film to watch, despite its sentimental ending. Pal's special effects are, as usual, superb, and completely carry the story. Characterization is rather weak, and one gets the impression that the movie was put together to feature effects, rather than people. Wells's version, of course, is considerably more thought-provoking than the screen affair, but Pal makes a credible presentation. Worth seeing once.

Based on an old American legend of an amphibious man, **The Creature from the Black Lagoon** (Universal, 1954), and its two sequels, **Revenge of the Creature** (Universal, 1955) and **The Creature Walks among Us** (Universal, 1956), feature the fascinating presence of the Gill Man (played by Ricou Browning). The discovery of a strange fossil hand in the Amazon basin prompts an expedition to the dark lagoon where it was discovered. As the four scientists begin their investigation, several members of the party are murdered. Dr. Reed (Richard Carlson) learns that a living Gill Man is responsible for the deaths, and he captures the creature by using a sleep drug. But the amphibian escapes, and blocks the exit from the lagoon. As the men try to dislodge the logjam, the Gill creature kidnaps Kay Lawrence (Julia Adams), and takes her to his underwater grotto. The remaining scientists follow the amphibian in scuba gear, confronting it in its lair, with spear guns and bullets. The wounded creature plunges back into the watery depths from which it sprang.

In **Revenge of the Creature**, Director Jack Arnold takes us back to the lagoon, where the creature is captured by scientist Clete Ferguson (John Agar), and removed to an aquarium in

The Gill Man, from *Revenge of the Creature* (Universal, 1955).

Florida. But the Gill Man enjoys his captivity no more than he did the first time around, and soon he escapes, kidnapping Clete's assistant, Helen Dobson (Lori Nelson). Naturally, the scientist rescues the girl, and the amphibian flees back to his watery lair amidst the customary spattering of bullets.

The Creature Walks Among Us features a different director (Jack Sherwood), and a new twist. After fleeing from Ferguson, the creature has reached the open seas off the coast of Florida, apparently headed for its Amazon homeland. A group of scientists follow the Gill Man's tracks, pursuing it into the Everglades, where it turns on them, and confronts them on their own boat. At the last moment, one of the men douses it with a kerosene lamp. The amphibian is seriously burned, and converted by an operation into a land creature, a mockery of both the human and fishman forms. In the end, of course, it escapes, wreaking the usual damage upon man and his creations, and staggers into the water, filled with bullets.

The Gill Man is a wholly unique creation, a perfect blend of man and fish, a creature who actually seems suited to his watery environment. Ricou Browning managed to bring a certain amount of pathos to the amphibian, who is continually hounded by scientists, driven from his tranquil, fish-eating existence, poked at and picked at in the name of progress. Once again, man the rapacious manages to destroy the works of nature.

Them! (Warner Brothers, 1954) features giant ants in the leading role. After several savage attacks on desert trailers, Police Officer Ben Peterson (James Whitmore) is called to investigate. The murdered victims are filled with formic acid, from which Peterson deduces that huge ants are involved. A helicopter search of the desert reveals their nest, and entomologists suggest poison.

One of the giant ants from *Them!* (Warner, 1954).

Three scenes from the Walt Disney production of *20,000 Leagues Under the Sea* (1954), adapted from the Jules Verne novel. (top) Captain Nemo's fantastic submarine, the "Nautilus"; (top right) the crew of the "Nautilus" bury one of their own in a moving undersea ceremony conducted by Captain Nemo; (bottom right) the attack of the giant squid endangers the ship, and the crew rushes to its defense. © Walt Disney Productions 1954.

The creatures are saturated with fumes, and most of them die underground. One queen escapes, however, making a nest in the Los Angeles sewer system. The army is called in, and storms through the tunnels, burning the ants with flame-throwers.

Them! is better wrought than most of its genre, but the limitations of the monster gimmick are evident throughout. The premise, that the creature's huge size was caused by atomic testing and radiation, is patently ridiculous. The ants themselves are credible creations, thoroughly menacing in their emotionless rapacity. A mediocre film, but in its mediocrity a hundred times better than most of its insectile successors.

20,000 Leagues Under the Sea (Buena Vista, 1954) was Walt Disney's first venture into science fiction, and the third screen version of Jules Verne's novel. In 1868, Captain Nemo (James Mason) has invented a fantastic undersea craft powered by atomic energy, and has vowed to abolish war by sinking the war ships of the world until the nations agree to his demands. Professor Aronnax (Paul Lukas) is a passenger of a ship dispatched to look for a strange sea beast reported in the South Pacific. Nemo sinks the vessel, and rescues Aronnax, his assistant Conseil (Peter Lorre), and harpoonist Ned Land (Kirk Douglas). Mason explains his mission, and shows them

around the futuristic craft. Disney's submarine is the perfect embodiment of Verne's vision, a mixture of the archaic and futuristic, a nineteenth century thing of wonder. The "Nautilus" is attacked by a giant squid, and Nemo is trapped until Ned lends a hand. Nemo is persuaded by Aronnax to give his secret of atomic energy to the world, in exchange for world disarmament. Aronnax will take Nemo's demands to the leaders of the world. However, Nemo's secret base has been located through a bottle note dropped by the refugees, and the allied armada surrounds his island hideaway. After letting the three companions go, Nemo fights his final battle, destroying his base and the allied ships in a huge explosion. The "Nautilus" plummets to the ocean floor, taking Nemo with it.

20,000 Leagues suffers from the usual Disney faults: sentimentalization, stereotyped characters, and a gushy wholesomeness that threatens, at times, to overwhelm the picture in mediocrity. What saves the film are the superior special effects (the fight with the giant squid is noteworthy in itself), the interesting portrayal of Nemo's complex nature by actor James Mason, and Disney's

Exeter (Jeff Morrow), Cal Meacham (Rex Reason), and Ruth Adams (Faith Domergue) are menaced by one of the insectoid mutants of Metaluna.—*This Island Earth* (Universal, 1955).

submarine. The underwater shots are particularly well-rendered. With an enormous budget for its time ($5 million), **20,000 Leagues Under the Sea** should have been the major SF film of its decade. It remains an entertaining, if slightly dated, piece of cinematography.

On the far-off planet of Metaluna, scientists are waging a desperate battle with the invading Zahgons. Such is the premise of **This Island Earth** (Universal, 1955), based on the novel of the same name by Raymond F. Jones. One of Metaluna's scientists, Exeter (Jeff Morrow), comes to Earth to obtain the uranium his planet needs to reinforce its gradually collapsing force fields. The force fields are necessary to ward off the unceasing rain of missiles being hailed down on the planet by the Zahgons. Exeter recruits a team of Earth scientists at his Georgia estate, including Cal Meacham (Rex Reason) and Ruth Adams (Faith Domergue).

As the situation decays on Metaluna, Exeter is ordered home by his superiors, and told to bring what little uranium he has. The two researchers flee in a small plane, which is scooped up by the alien's flying saucer. But Exeter arrives too late to save his planet, as Zahgon missiles begin penetrating the screens. The giant, insectile mutants who serve the scientists revolt against their masters, contributing to the chaos. The Metalunans' plans to immigrate to Earth are thwarted by Exeter, who shepherds the humans through the falling debris, back aboard the interstellar craft. At the last moment, an insect mutant slips through the door, seriously wounding the Metalunan. Exeter manages to pilot his ship back to Earth, where he releases Cal and Ruth in their airplane, before plunging his craft into a fiery dive into the sea.

Joseph Newman, Director of **This Island Earth**, deserves much credit for his sensitive handling of the alien theme. The Metalunans are put in a philosophical quandary, which ultimately resolves itself in favor of the Earthlings. Jeff Morrow's portrayal of Exeter is quiet and effective,

Victor Carron (Richard Wordsworth) turns into a cactus.—*The Quatermass Xperiment* (1955).

Quatermass II (also called *Enemy from Space*) once again featured Brian Donlevy as Professor Quatermass.

a man from outer space with more scruples than his Earthly companions. The scenes on the alien planet are spectacular. One feels genuine sympathy for the unfortunate Metalunans, who are waging a hopeless war, and know it. Worth at least a single look.

   Nigel Kneale produced three six-part television series for the British Broadcasting Corporation during the 1950s; all three featured a rocket scientist named Quatermass, and all three were later made into movies. **The Quatermass Xperiment** (Exclusive, 1955), also released in the United States as **The Creeping Unknown,** featured Brian Donlevy in the title role. The first manned space

Godzilla (Toho, 1954, and Embassy, 1956) destroys Tokyo harbor.

flight returns to Earth with only one of its three astronauts, Victor Carroon (Richard Wordsworth), still alive. Quatermass is called in to investigate the strange mystery. Gradually, Carroon is being possessed by an alien disease that alters his human appearance. The creature within him has the power to absorb the bodies of those it touches. In the end, the loathsome mass that was once Victor Carroon is electrocuted by high tension wires, and the menace from outer space is destroyed.

The second film in the series, **Quatermass II** (Anglo-Amalgamated, 1957), also called **Enemy from Space** in the U. S., featured the same team as the first picture, including Brian Donlevy and Director Val Guest. Aliens from "out there" invade the lonely British countryside in small, rocket-shaped meteorites. The rocks burst open when picked up, releasing the forces within; their human victims are immediately taken over by these superior intelligences. The professor investigates, and triumphs in the end, as we might expect.

Neither of these films holds up very well a second time around. The special effects are shoddily done, and the acting is mediocre. Of the two, **The Quatermass Xperiment** seems more convincing, but just barely. The third movie in the sequence, **Quatermass and the Pit (Five Million Years to Earth**), was made in 1967, with a different set of stars and a new technical crew, and is

(above) *Satellite in the Sky* (Warner, 1956) featured the testing of a ''tritonium bomb'' in orbit; the bomb fails to jettison, and will destroy the ship and its crew unless an answer can be found.

(below) Miles Bennell (Kevin McCarthy) discovers one of the alien pods growing in his neighbor's garden.—*Invasion of the Body Snatchers* (Allied Artists, 1956).

generally regarded as the best of the lot. A fuller review of this film is provided in a later section of this book.

Godzilla (Toho, 1954, but spliced with extra footage for its 1956 American release) was the first of an unending series of Japanese-made horror and monster films. America's nuclear tests in the Pacific release a dinosaur-like creature from its centuries-long prison on the ocean floor. Godzilla wreaks massive destruction on ships and minor Japanese islands, and then heads for Tokyo. Steve Martin (Raymond Burr), a reporter for an American news service, watches the story develop from his headquarters in Tokyo. After trampling half the city into the ground, the monster returns to the sea. In despair, the government calls upon a Japanese scientist, who has invented a device that consumes all oxygen in the water. The weapon works, and Godzilla falls apart in a pile of bones.

The Burr sequences were added by Embassy Pictures, which bought the movie for American distribution. **Godzilla** was an enormous commercial success in both the United States and Japan, and unfortunately spawned several dozen sequels and imitations from the Japanese film industry, many of them featuring the resurrected creature itself.

1956 was by far the best year for science fiction films in the middle and later part of the Fifties, producing three pictures of distinction. **Invasion of the Body Snatchers** (Allied Artists, 1956), a quiet, underplayed drama of the aliens among us, was adapted from Jack Finney's novel of the same title. Dr. Miles Bennell (Kevin McCarthy) returns home from vacation to the small California town of Santa Mira. During his absence, a strange hysteria has spread through the townsfolk, and many of the people seem passive and emotionless to Bennell. Miles and his former girlfriend, Becky Driscoll (Dana Wynter), are called to the house of Jack Velichec (King Donovan), who has found a giant pod of some sort in his greenhouse. The pod is turning into a likeness of Velichec. When it comes alive, the men realize that they are facing an insidious alien invasion, in which the pods are gradually replacing humans, taking over their minds while they sleep, and destroying the original bodies. The resulting automatons are passive, emotionless, ambitionless, and partially telepathic. Bennell tries to contact the authorities, but the whole town has been taken over, with the exception of Becky and himself. Suddenly, the townsmen come after them, in a chilling sequence where Miles and Becky are chased through the village streets by the entire population of Santa Mira. But the reunited lovers manage to escape their hunters, and hole up in a cave, where Becky falls asleep from exhaustion. The girl is possessed by the pods, and suddenly turns on Bennell; the doctor is forced to flee for his life. Picked up by the police for drunkenness, Miles is taken to a Los Angeles hospital, where he tells his story in flashbacks. But no one believes him, until a highway accident spills a load of pods onto the road. The FBI is contacted, and mankind may yet be saved.

Little regarded at the time it was released, **Invasion of the Body Snatchers** has gained a considerable reputation among critics in the ensuing years. McCarthy is superbly cast as a sensitive man forced to cope with horrors beyond his experience. Don Siegel, Director of **Invasion**, purposely focused his camera directly on the differences between the controlled townsmen and those still free from domination. The real horror is the destruction of the individual, the dissipation of the emotions that distinguish men from animals (or aliens). Siegel's film is a classic parable of one man trying to preserve the values that make life worth living.

The screen version of **1984** (Holiday, 1956) is a watered-down version of George Orwell's terrifying vision of tomorrow. Winston Smith (Edmond O'Brien) works for the government of Oceania, one of the three great world states of 1984. Smith's job is revising history, as recorded in books and periodicals of the past, to reflect the changing political whims of his government.

(above)   General O'Connor (Michael Redgrave) inspects propagandists at work revising history, in *1984* (Holiday, 1956).

(right)   Robbie the Robot, the mechanical wonder of Altair IV, stands guard over the *Forbidden Planet* (MGM, 1956).

Like most of the citizens of this totalitarian state, Smith lives in low-class housing, an apartment complex continually monitored by telescreens (two-way TV sets), which can be turned down, but never actually shut off.

Smith falls in love with Julia (Jan Sterling), an emotion forbidden by the State; the lovers bitterly resent the government's interference in the private lives of its citizens, and vow to overthrow Big Brother, the ever-present image of the party leader.   General O'Connor (Michael Redgrave) seems to be sympathetic to their schemes, but is actually an undercover agent who

106

turns them in. The lovers' final rendezvous point is the back room of an old pawnshop, where they are captured by government agents. Two endings were filmed: in one, Smith and Julia are killed as they scream their defiance; in the other, more faithful rendering, Winston and his lover are brainwashed by the Thought Police into renouncing their love for each other.

Michael Anderson, the film's Director, chose to downplay Orwell's uncompromising picture of a ruthless, heartless, cruel society which will stop at nothing to keep its citizens under complete mental and moral control. He thereby sacrificed some of the movie's effectiveness for a more palatable screen image. The most horrifying scenes are precisely those which adhere most faithfully to the original: the five-minute "hate," the brainwashing of Smith and Julia, the sterile pictures of a future London that is all dust and concrete. And while the film remains a chilling visual experience, the definitive version has yet to be made.

Forbidden Planet (Metro-Goldwyn-Mayer, 1956) is one of the better science fiction films of its day, a loose adaption of Shakespeare's final play, **The Tempest**. A space patrol is sent to investigate a missing expedition on the planet Altair IV. Commander Adams (Leslie Nielsen) and his military crew land their craft near the sole settlement, despite the warnings of Dr. Morbius (Walter Pidgeon). Morbius and his daughter are the sole survivors of the colony, the others having been killed shortly after their arrival by strange unseen monsters. Morbius tells the commander that the creatures vanished immediately after the killings, and he and his daughter have lived in peace ever since. Altaira Morbius (Anne Francis) has never seen any humans but her father, and the presence of so many young men fascinates her. A romance springs up between her and Adams.

Meanwhile, strange things have been happening back at the spaceship, and there are signs that the invisible monster of old has returned. When several of the crew are killed, Adam orders an electrical fence set up around the craft. The fence stops the creature momentarily, outlining it in horrific detail: the monster is a huge cross between a lion and a bull. Then the strands shatter, and several more men are killed before the thing departs. Adams is determined to solve the mystery, and he forces Morbius to tell him the secret of the planet. Eons before, Altair had been inhabited by the Krell, a race as far in advance of man as man is over the ape. The Krell had hollowed out vast caverns in their world, and filled them with mile upon mile of computers. The culmination of their civilization was the development of a machine that could synthesize matter from thought. Not realizing the extent of their own hidden bestiality, the Krell literally vanished overnight, as they were ravaged by the monsters of their own subconscious minds.

Adams realizes suddenly that the invisible creature is Morbius's unconscious creation; Morbius has spent many years tampering with the Krell machines, trying to make them function. Morbius refuses to believe Adam's theory, until the monster besieges the trio in the Krell control

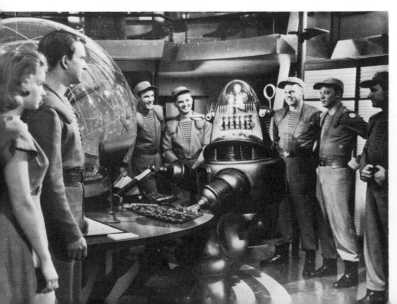

(left) Altaira (Anne Francis) and Adams (Leslie Nielsen) watch Robbie manipulate the controls of Adams's space ship.—*Forbidden Planet* (MGM, 1956).

(below) *The Mysterians* (Toho, 1957) seek to enslave Earth with their giant robot. They fail.

The dead ymir, from *20 Million Miles to Earth* (Columbia, 1957).

center. As the invisible being burns its way through two feet of the Krell's indestructible metal, Adams points to the dials around them, showing bank after bank of computer sections coming to the assistance of the invisible thing. Convinced at last, Morbius defeats the being from his subconscious by absorbing it into his mind; he then pushes a button that will destroy the planet completely within 24 hours. Altaira is told to leave with Adams, and together, they watch the planet disintegrate from the vantage point of outer space.

Forbidden Planet featured superior special effects, the first "cute" robot (Robby) to appear on the screen, and an intelligent and thought-provoking premise. In retrospect, however, the film appears somewhat dated, perhaps because the characterizations are so typical of the Fifties. The girl is completely naive, the soldiers are boyishly flippant, and Morbius is suitably morose. Also, the sets are rather flat (the movie was filmed entirely on sound stages). **Forbidden Planet** is still an interesting film, but not the best of its time, as some critics have claimed.

20 Million Miles to Earth (Columbia, 1957) is a very minor film noteworthy only for the superb animation of Ray Harryhausen. The first manned flight to Venus returns to a crash-landing off the coast of Italy. Only one of the astronauts, Col. Calder (William Hopper), survives. Calder had brought back with him the egg of an ymir, a dinosaur-like creature on Venus. The egg is washed ashore on the Italian coast, picked up by a small boy, and sold to a zoologist, Dr. Leonardo (Frank Puglia). Soon, the egg hatches, and the foot-long creature that emerges begins growing at a rapid rate. After a brief period in the Rome zoo, the ymir, now as big as the elephant it fights and kills, makes its way to the top of the Coliseum, where the army destroys the beast, together with the city's main tourist attraction. Man is saved again from an alien menace.

This tiresome rehashing of worn-out plots does have one redeeming quality, the ymir itself. Beautifully rendered by Harryhausen, the beast is absolutely convincing as an alien creature, comparing favorably with his exquisite work in the later Sinbad films. An interesting visual experience.

The Incredible Shrinking Man (Universal, 1957) is the classic screen rendition of man in miniature. Scott Carey (Grant Williams) is sailing with his wife when their boat passes through a strange cloud of mist. Carey is the only one on deck at the time. A few months later, Carey finds himself growing progressively shorter, at a steady and irreversible rate. Doctors and scientists alike are befuddled by his retrogression, and can do nothing to reverse it. Meanwhile, Scott's wife is finding her husband's notoriety increasingly difficult to cope with, and begins treating her pint-sized spouse like a child.

After a brief affair with a female midget, Scott is sequestered in a doll house, where he is besieged by the family cat, knocked down the basement stairs, and effectively lost to humanity thereafter. By this time, Carey is only three inches tall; unable to climb the steps back to the main part of the house, and unable to make himself heard, Scott must learn to fend for himself. After fighting off a spider (which he kills with a pin), the shrinking man walks through the screen of the basement window into the garden, philosophically musing that he is still alive, that there must be some purpose to it all.

Scripted by Richard Matheson from his novel of the same name, **The Incredible Shrinking Man** is an intelligent and sensitive portrayal of a man forced to survive under impossible odds. Ironically, as the film progresses, and Carey grows ever smaller, his character grows larger: he discovers his own worth, and gradually matures into a strong, capable human being. At the end, when his size threatens to plunge him down to the microscopic level, Carey has come to terms with himself, and is ready to face whatever may lie on the other side of the grate, with courage and understanding.

Clifford Stine's special effects are beautifully proportioned to William's ever-changing size. Director Jack Arnold deserves particular credit for keying the story to man, rather than the gimmick of miniaturization; each trial that Carey faces adds to his personal stature, as he is forced to feel the ultimate loneliness of being the only member of his species left at his particular size. Arnold's movie is a superior piece of cinematography, second only to **The Day the Earth Stood Still** as the best SF film of the decade.

(top right)   Brett Halsey as Philippe Delambre in *Return of the Fly* (Twentieth Century-Fox, 1959).

(right)   Scott Carey (Grant Williams) defends himself from a tarantula, in *The Incredible Shrinking Man* (Universal, 1957).

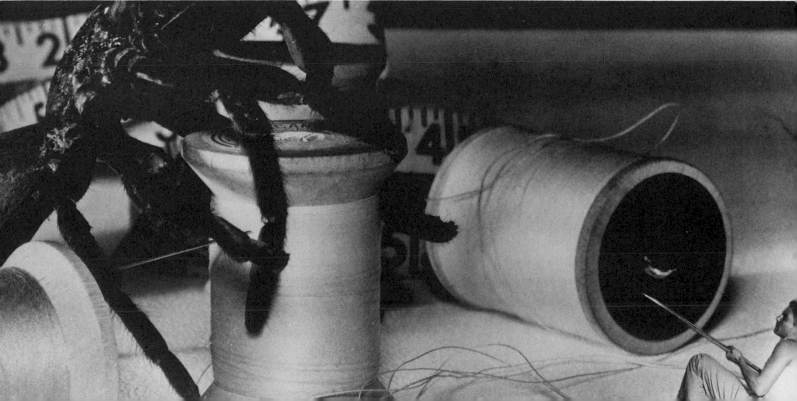

In **The Fly** (Twentieth Century-Fox, 1958), Andre Delambre (David Hedison) invents a matter projector, and accidentally gets the head and arm of a fly when he tries to transmit himself through the machine. The fly, which had found its way into the box unnoticed by Delambre, now has his head and arm, and Andre must locate the insect to have any hope of recovering his normal body. Meanwhile, the fly's personality is beginning to exert its influence on the scientist's body and Delambre asks his wife Helene (Patricia Owens) for help, but to no avail. Fearing that his fly brain will take over completely, Andre finally asks Helene to kill him in such a way as to leave no trace of his appendages. They find his body crushed beneath a hydraulic press. The police investigate, and Helene tells her story in flashbacks. Unimpressed, the Inspector walks in the garden with Francois Delambre (Vincent Price), Andre's brother. There they hear a small, piping voice shouting, "Help me!" The fly with Andre's head has been caught in a spider web. Price kills the fly with a rock.

Although better than most of its ilk, **The Fly**, adapted from the story by George Langelaan,

From the Earth to the Moon (Warner, 1958) featured Joseph Cotten as the inventer of a powerful explosive that propels the first space craft around the Moon.

Pat Boone takes a moment to rest from his *Journey to the Center of the Earth* (Twentieth Century-Fox, 1959).

still leaves much to be desired. The transmitter is unconvincing, and so is the premise of the story, that Delambre still retains enough of his own personality to be worried about life as an insect. The movie was enough of a commerical success to spawn two sequels, **Return of the Fly** (1959), and **Curse of the Fly** (1965), which employ the same gimmick in less convincing fashion.

Following on the success of **20,000 Leagues Under the Sea** (1954), Twentieth Century-Fox filmed a "wholesome" version of another Verne classic, **Journey to the Center of the Earth** (1959). Professor Oliver Lindenbrook (James Mason) is honored with the gift of a paperweight by his students. The rock turns out to be a message from an explorer who has penetrated to the Earth's core. Mason uses the markings to pinpoint the entrance to the caverns, and mounts an expedition to Iceland, where the caves begin. Together with his student Alex McEwan (Pat Boone), a guide named Hans (Peter Ronson), and Carla (Arlene Dahl), the widow of an old friend and fellow scientist, Lindenbrook finds the opening, and they begin their descent.

Following in their footsteps is Count Saknussemm (Thayer David), who wants to claim the glory of the discovery for himself. After passing through a field of giant mushrooms, the explorers come to a vast sea, where they build a raft, and set sail. The Count is killed, and the Lindenbrook party is forced to fight off dinosaurs and the other prehistoric beasts which have survived beneath the Earth's surface. The exit shaft, located near the ruins of Atlantis, is blocked by a boulder. The Professor blows the stone apart with dynamite, igniting an ancient volcano. The survivors climb onto a giant Atlantean bowl, and are pushed by a column of lava up through the volcano of Stromboli, in Italy.

Journey to the Center of the Earth is juvenile fare by today's standards, filled with hackneyed plot situations, mediocre special effects (the ''dinosaurs'' are dressed-up lizards). and cardboard characters. Pat Boone, in particular, is rather insipid in his wholesomeness. So typical of its time, **Journey** is not a bad film, but not a very good one either.

The Fifties closed with a remarkable film that was never touted as science fiction, but most certainly is. **On the Beach** (United Artists, 1959), scripted from the novel by Nevil Shute (pseudonym of Nevil Shute Norway, who died a year later), tells the story of mankind's inglorious end. A nuclear war devastates the northern hemisphere, leaving Australia and South America intact, but doomed to inevitable extinction when the radiation clouds move south. Gregory Peck is Commander Dwight Towers, Captain of America's last submarine, the ''Sawfish.'' Peck is delegated to investigate a radio message being received from the San Francisco area. The Australians have hopes that someone may still survive on the ravaged North American continent.

As expected, however, the irregular signal is caused by natural forces (the wind), and there are no signs of life anywhere. Peck returns to Melbourne, where the Aussies begin choosing their deaths. Some, like scientist Julian Osborn (Fred Astaire), participate in reckless automobile races, hoping to smash themselves in one final act of glory. Others take suicide pills to avoid the extended agonies of radiation poisoning. Peck finds solace with Moira Davidson (Ava Gardner), but then is forced to separate from her when his crew chooses to die at home. The final scenes of the picture feature the stark, empty streets of Melbourne, festooned with an evangelist's banner: ''There is still time, brother.''

On the Beach is an uncompromising picture of the human race committing suicide, and wishing bitterly and regretfully it had some other choice. But man makes a dignified end, perhaps too dignified; one wonders at times whether we would really go as quietly and gracefully as Producer/Director Stanley Kramer depicts. On the whole, however, **On the Beach** is a forceful affirmation of the beauty of life, and a harsh condemnation of the follies of nuclear brinksmanship. Nicely done.

MONOLiTHS ANO MONKEYS

(1960-1969)

The Sixties mark a turning point in the history of the science fiction film. Prior to this time, science fiction was just another genre category to the small and medium movie companies who occasionally ventured into fantastic cinema. On the whole, these early SF pictures shared the all-too-common defects of shoddy production values, poor scripting, virtually identical plots ("the monster is among us," "aliens from outer space," "beware of the flying saucers," etc.), low budgets, terrible acting and actors, and phony special effects. The occasional outstanding film only served to highlight the abysmal levels of the rest. SF films were aimed primarily at the "kiddie" market, the teens and sub-teens who frequented the "B" movie halls. No one invested much money into any one film, because none of the producers had expectations of making very much back. The audiences, being mostly young, demanded very little in the way of sophistication in return.

All of this changed in the 1960s. For the first time, film-makers began taking a serious look at the genre's possiblities, and began investing enough money on special effects to make some of their imaginings believable and real. The 1960s saw the first $10 million dollar science fiction film, **2001: A Space Odyssey**, an enormous financial and creative success. The growth of the genre in motion pictures paralleled the gradual acceptance of science fiction literature during this same period, matched with an awakening interest in the field from the academic world, and increasing

(bottom) The Time Traveller (Rod Taylor) prepares to set out on his journey through the ages, in George Pal's *The Time Machine* (MGM, 1960), an adaptation of H. G. Wells's novel.

(right) Weena (Yvette Mimieux) is caught by a Morlock.—*The Time Machine*.

sales of SF books, particularly paperbacks. During the 1960s, science fiction emerged from its long dark age into a new renaissance, a harbinger of things to come.

George Pal's **The Time Machine** (Metro-Goldwyn-Mayer, 1960), was a loose adaptation of H. G. Wells's novel of the same name. On New Year's Eve, 1899, the Time Traveller calls together a group of his London friends to demonstrate his new invention, a miniature version of a machine that will travel through time. The scientists are skeptical when the device disappears, and the Time Traveller (Rod Taylor) promises to bring them evidence that his invention really works. The time machine is a thing of glory, filled with crystalline bars, whirling dials, and a large, circular metallic backdrop, like a painted Oriental gong. The sequence where Taylor first tries out his machine is perhaps the most effective part of the film; slowly, we watch the world change, as the laboratory clock moves quickly forward, the candles melt, and the sun and moon traverse the sky in less than a minute of objective time. Soon, the passing of the days and nights are no more than flashes of light and dark. The Time Traveller stops briefly in 1914 and 1941, where he is disturbed to find the world at war. His third visit, in 1966, nearly ends his journey; an atomic war breaks out, destroying London, and releasing a lava flow which swamps his machine; he manages to throw the knob forward just in time.

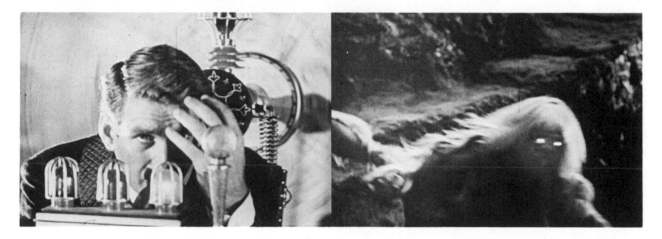

By the time the lava hill erodes, and he can escape from his prison of stone, hundreds of centuries have passed; the year is 802,701, and a new order has arisen. On the surface of what used to be England live the Eloi, timid, gentle folk who spend their lives in idle leisure, virtually unable to take care of themselves. Beneath the surface, in hollowed-out caverns, are the Morlocks, descendants of the factory workers, shaggy, white degenerates who flee from light, and who raise the Eloi as cattle. Neither group has much appeal, but Weena (played by Yvette Mimieux), an Eloi, at least looks human, in her own beautiful way; naturally, the Time Traveller takes up her cause. After fighting off the local band of Morlocks, and saving Weena from becoming just another meal, Taylor returns to London to meet again with his fellow scientists. But he has no proof of his story, save one fragile blossom of a flower unknown to man; so, gathering up a few books, the Time Traveller runs back to his laboratory. A strange whirring sound is heard, and there, where the time machine had once stood, are empty tracks in the snow. Producer/Director Pal made effective use of stop-action techniques in making travel through time a reality; but the atomic war sequence in ''1966'' destroys the credibility of the film for the contemporary viewer.

Based on John Wyndham's novel, **The Midwich Cuckoos, Village of the Damned** (Metro-Goldwyn-Mayer, 1960) is a quiet tale of horror in a small English village. Midwich is rendered

118

(far left)   Rod Taylor peers intently at *The Time Machine* (1960).

(near left)   The Morlocks, like most creatures of the night, have eyes that glow.

(above)   The Time Traveller fights the Morlocks in their underground lair, their ancient machines pounding in the background.—*The Time Machine* (MGM, 1960).

immobile by an unseen alien force, and when the villagers awake, they find every woman of child-bearing age pregnant. The children born of this unnatural union exhibit unusual powers, communicating with each other mentally, and using their telepathic abilities to control those around them. Their ultimate end seems to be control of the world. One man, Dr. Zellaby (played by George Sanders) takes a scientific interest in the children, and is admitted into their closed circle. After studying their remarkable powers and intelligence, he concludes that the children must be eliminated if mankind is to survive. By lecturing them on their responsibility to the world, he holds their collective attention long enough for dynamite to be placed in the schoolhouse. Suddenly, Zellaby's son David, the leader of the mutants, realizes what is happening, and moves to stop it; but the dynamite explodes, and Zellaby and the children are killed. The film's slow pace and low-key action make it a particularly effective study of man versus his mental superior. A sequel, **Children of the Damned** (1963), is very similar in many respects, but less effective.

Master of the World (American International, 1961) features Robur the Conqueror, from the Jules Verne novel of the same name. Like Captain Nemo, Robur is a master inventor, who con-

David (Martin Stephens) is the leader of the super-intelligent children in the *Village of the Damned* (MGM, 1960).

structs a nineteenth century powered flying machine, and with it terrorizes the world. Robur (Vincent Price) hates war, and his solution to man's eternal plague is the destruction of earth's armies and weapons, by bombing them from the skies. Paradoxically, this mad genius fights war by waging war. In the end, a government agent (Charles Bronson) destroys the "Albatross" by planting explosives, and Robur goes down in the flames of his own megalomania. Like **The Time Machine**, the "Albatross" is an interesting combination of the old and the new, a genuinely futuristic craft constructed from an archaic point of view. The story itself is basically the same as Verne's earlier book, **20,000 Leagues Under the Sea**.

Almost all the science fiction films produced in modern times have been full-length features; shorter flicks are rare, and good shorts are rarer still. **La Jetee** (Argos, 1962), only lasts for half an hour, but in that space of time manages to pack in more things of interest than most of its longer brothers and sisters. Paris has been destroyed by an atomic bomb. The few survivors eke out an existence in underground caverns beneath the city. Their only hope of survival is contact with the

120

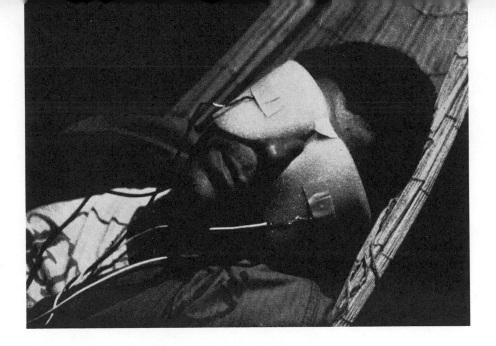

(above)   Davos Henich, the masked time traveller of *La Jetee* (Argos, 1962).

(below)   Vincent Price stars as Robur the Conqueror, in *Master of the World*, from Jules Verne's novel of the same name (American International, 1961).

future; the unnamed protagonist (Davos Henich) is chosen for the initial experiment in time travel because of his recurring nightmare, an actual memory from his childhood in which he saw a man shot down at Orly Airport, near the feet of a young woman. After repeated chemical injections, the hero makes contact with the girl, projecting himself physically into the past, and eventually falling in love with her.

(left)   The Triffids, giant, ambulatory plants with stingers, are out to get mankind, in *The Day of the Triffids* (Allied Artists, 1963).

(below)   One of the radioactive children.—*The Damned* (Columbia, 1963).

Having proved time travel possible, the scientists of the catacombs want Henich to reach an advanced race of the far future. He does, moving into the future through a network of lines in a picture. Having completed his mission, the hero retreats again into his past, running backwards in time towards the image of the girl, as she looms before him on the airport jetty. Just before he reaches her waiting arms, he realizes what is happening, and turns around to see himself shot down by one of the scientists from his own time. Nearby, a little child looks in horror. Chris Marker, director of the film, achieved notable effects by depicting the entire film in stills (save for one very brief segment near its end), with narration overlaid. The picture had almost no circulation in the United States, although it has been shown several times on Public Broadcasting System stations.

Like **The Thing**, covered in an earlier section of this book, **The Day of the Triffids** (Allied Artists, 1963) menaces mankind with walking vegetables. A meteor shower on Earth causes most of the population (those who watched it) to permanently lose their sight. Bill Masen (Howard Keel) is recovering from an eye operation; he awakens on the morning after the shower to find London deserted. After locating a sighted child, and realizing the extent of the disaster, he crosses the Channel to France. During the shower, seeds had been dropped from the skies, and now the Triffids, seven-foot moving plants with poisonous stingers, are rounding up and killing the remnants of mankind. Two marine biologists, isolated in a lighthouse, finally discover the creatures' weak point, dissolving them with salt (sea) water. Mankind is saved, but civilization is in ruins. This interesting parable, adapted from the novel by John Wyndham, had some serious flaws, but still remains one of the better "menace-from-outer-space" flicks.

Little known in the United States, **The Damned** (Columbia, 1963), also released in abridged form as **These Are the Damned**, is perhaps the one outstanding film dealing with the menace of atomic warfare. While fleeing from a motorcycle gang, Simon Wells (Macdonald Carey) and Joan (Shirley Ann Field) stumble into a sea cave surrounded by barbed wire, and inhabited by nine very lonely children. Wells is astonished to learn that the children have never seen adult humans in the flesh; all their needs are supplied by automatons, various delivery systems and men in protective suits. Determined to expose the government's tampering with the lives of these innocents, Simon and Joan prepare to leave.

But the television screen comes to life, and Bernard (Alexander Knox), the scientist in charge of the project, explains the situation: these nine children have been systematically exposed to radiation, so that, in the event of a nuclear war, some small portion of the species will be able to survive. Meanwhile, Simon and Joan attempt to leave. The lovers set out from the cliff in a small boat, closely monitored by a government helicopter. But no effort is made to stop them. The children are themselves radioactive, and Simon and Joan have been around them so long that they too are doomed; the government need only wait. The little parable of governmental immorality, adapted from the novel **Children of Light**, by H. L. Lawrence, is a cold-blooded indictment of bureaucratic thinking and planning. The humanity of the principals is never a factor in the government's considerations.

Dr. Strangelove; or, How I Learned to Stop Worrying and Love the Bomb (Columbia, 1963), based on Peter Bryant's novel, **Red Alert**, was Stanley Kubrick's first great success. Starring Peter Sellers in three roles, as Strangelove, President Muffley, and Group Captain Lionel Mandrake, the film tells the story of General Jack D. Ripper (Sterling Hayden), who seals off the airbase he commands, and orders a fleet of B-52 Bombers to strike the Soviet Union. The army is forced to storm the base, and Ripper commits suicide, taking the recall codes with him; Col. Mandrake, however, manages to decipher the code from the General's papers. Unfortunately, one

The American War Room.—*Dr. Strangelove* (Columbia, 1963).

of the planes, commanded by T. J. "King" Kong (Slim Pickens) is damaged in the attack, and fails to respond. The Soviet Premier, Pistoff, tells Muffley that Russia has recently installed a Dooms-day Machine, which will automatically set off all the atom bombs in the world if the Soviet Union is attacked. The bomb is dropped, Slim Pickens riding it down all the way, and mankind comes to an inglorious end. Black comedy of the finest kind.

H. G. Wells has been a favorite subject for motion picture makers from the early days of the silents. **First Men in the Moon**, adapted from the novel of the same name, was first filmed in 1919 by Jack Leigh. The most recent version, produced in 1964 for Columbia Pictures by Charles Schneer and Ray Harryhausen, is an amusing exercise in nineteenth century pseudo-science fiction. Professor Cavor (Lionel Jeffries) discovers a new substance which nullifies gravity, and proposes to make a trip to the Moon in a vessel constructed with Cavorite shutters. Taking along Arnold Bedford (Edward Judd) and his fiance, Kate Callender (Martha Hyer), Cavor launches his spherical spaceship towards the Lunar plains. After making a successful landing, the trio discover a race of insect-like beings living in caverns beneath the Moon's surface.

The Selenites rescue the Earthlings from a giant Moon calf (caterpillar), and drag their captives before the Grand Lunar, who is half-insect and half-machine. Because of their war-like tendencies, the humans will not be allowed to leave, but Bedford and Kate rebel against the Lunar's decision, and fight their way back to the space craft. Cavor stays behind to study the Selenites further. Years later in 1965, the first manned flight to the Moon discovers a small British flag on the cratered surface, together with a piece of paper mentioning Bedford. Locating the old man in a rest home, the world gets the entire story of the Cavor expedition. But the Selenites themselves have vanished, as the modern-day astronauts soon find out: Cavor's cold germs apparently wiped them out. An amusing fantasy which doesn't take itself too seriously.

(preceding pages) Eight scenes from *First Men in the Moon* (Columbia, 1964): as viewed clockwise, Cavor's ship heads for the Moon; the intrepid astronauts explore the Lunar surface; a Moon flower; the Grand Lunar, entombed in his crystalline home; an insectoid Selenite; Cavor (Lionel Jeffries) is confronted by a Selenite; Cavor faces the long march to the throne of the Grand Lunar; a Moon calf (giant insect) menaces the Lunar party. *First Men in the Moon* was adapted by Charles Schneer and Ray Harryhausen from the novel by H. G. Wells.

(previous page) Christopher Draper (Paul Mantee) and his pet monkey Mona are stranded on a barren world, in *Robinson Crusoe on Mars* (Paramount, 1964).

Atragon (Toho, 1964) featured a craft which dives beneath the ocean, flies, and burrows into the Earth; this futuristic flying sub is the key in man's struggle against the Kingdom of Mu, a subterranean empire determined to conquer the world.

The Tenth Victim (Embassy, 1965), based upon Robert Sheckley's short story, "The Seventh Victim," presents another dystopian view of the future, where agressions are channeled into the "Hunt." Citizens of the 21st century may elect to enter the Hunt, a form of legalized murder, in which each participant must alternatively serve ten times as Hunter and Hunted. In each case, the Hunt is terminated by killing one's opponent. A citizen who has joined the Hunt may not withdraw, except through death. Anyone who survives ten kills attains a privileged status in society, with a lifetime pension, special political rights, and international fame.

The giant computer that arranges the matches assigns Marcello Polletti (Marcello Mastroianni) to be the tenth victim of Caroline Meredith (Ursula Andress). As is customary in these proceedings, the victim is merely notified that he is being hunted; Andress, however, is given a complete dossier on her subject. Andress arranges to have the final kill filmed for a television commercial, but Marcello escapes her trap. In the end, Caroline decides that love is better than money, and kidnaps Mastroianni by helicopter, flying him to a church where a priest is waiting. Marcello has a choice: submit or be killed; and being only human, he submits. Despite the fact that much of the film is played for laughs, with a particularly weak ending, **The Tenth Victim** does have moments to chill the spine; indeed, its very lightheartedness only serves to highlight the bloody business of kill-and-be-killed. With a tighter plot, and a little more attention to detail, this one could have been a classic.

Jean-Luc Godard has ventured on a number of science fiction excursions, including **Le Nouveau Monde** (1962), and **Alphaville; Une Etrange Aventure de Lemmy Caution** (1965), one of the most interesting of his films. In the future metropolis of Alphaville, ruled by the giant computer,

One of the bizarre costumes worn in the future world of *The Tenth Victim* (Embassy, 1965).

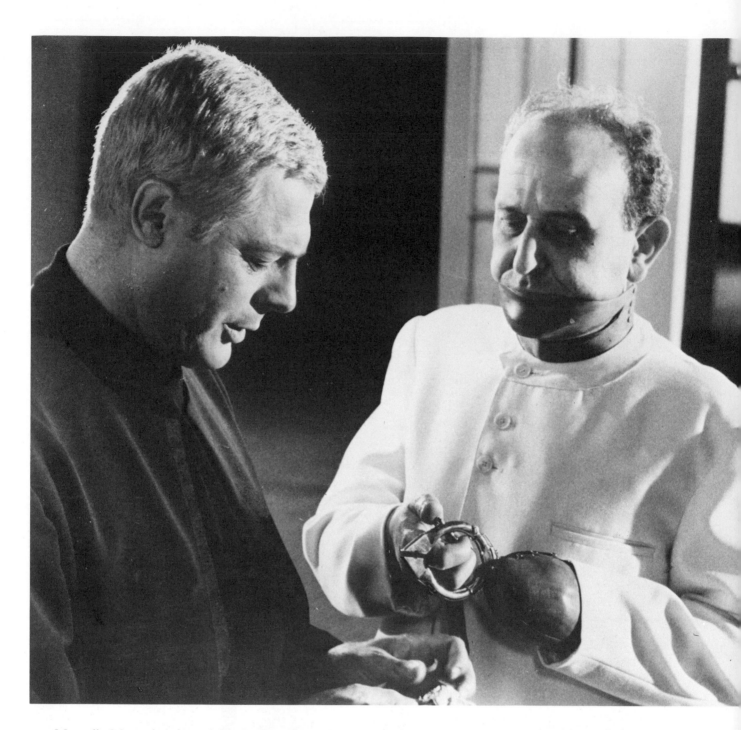

Marcello Mastroianni receiving instruction on how to defend his life, in *The Tenth Victim* (1965).

Alpha-60, secret agent Lemmy Caution (Eddie Constantine) is hunting his fellow agent, Henry Dickson (Akim Tamiroff), who has inexplicably vanished. In his wanderings, he encounters a beautiful young girl controlled by the computer, falls in love, frees her from the machine's domination, and escapes into the outer world, leaving Alphaville in chaos. Once again, man's illogic proves incomprehensible to the sensible computer, which is incapable of understanding the emotional side of humanity. Although the man-controlled-by-machine theme has become common, **Alphaville** remains a film worth seeing.

In **Fahrenheit 451** (Universal, 1966), even the credits are verbal. This dystopian world of the future, adapted by Francois Truffaut from Ray Bradbury's novel, features a totalitarian government which keeps the populace in check through complete control of the mass media. Books are banned: to own one is a major crime. A special fleet of firemen exists solely to burn whatever volumes are located. Newspapers are distributed in the comic book form, but most people spend their leisure time watching wall television sets, responding to questions fed directly to them from the tube. Montag (Oskar Werner) is a typical fireman; one day, while burning a treasure trove of books scavenged by an old woman, he sees the hag throw herself into the flames rather than part with her possessions. Intrigued, he smuggles a forbidden volume home, and begins reading.

His wife Linda (Julie Christie) fails to understand this new passion, and sticks with her TV set. But Clarisse (also Julie Christie), a girl he meets on the monorail, pushes him along the path to growth with her insidious question of "why." Inevitably, Montag is turned in by his wife, out of misguided loyalty to the state, and the firemen mark a path to his own door. But Montag is no longer the submissive minion that his government would have him be, and he turns on his fellow book-burners, incinerating them with their own flamethrowers. He and Clarisse escape to a rebel

The Firemen burn a hoard of illegal books, in Ray Bradbury's *Fahrenheit 451* (Universal, 1966).

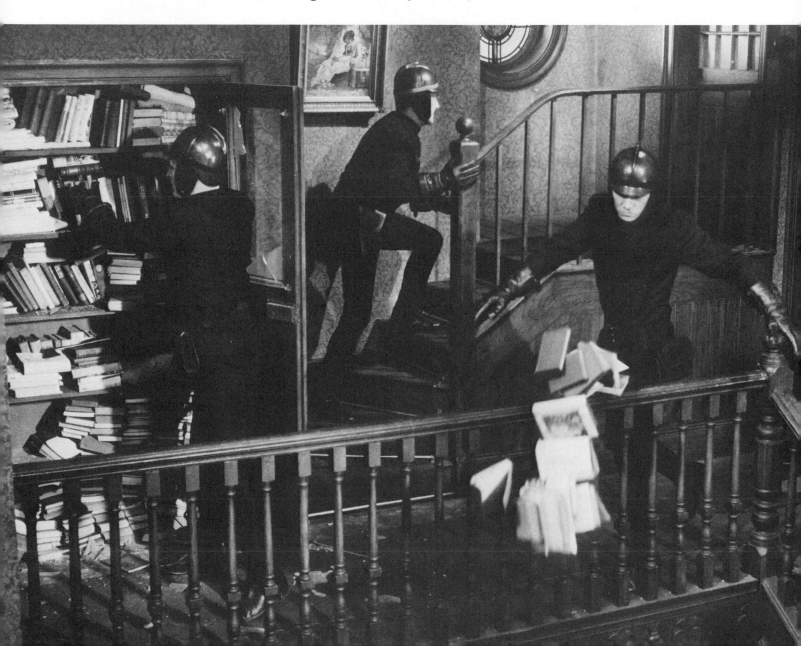

William Redfield, Raquel Welch, Arthur Kennedy, Donald Pleasance, and Stephen Boyd prepare to make their *Fantastic Voyage* into a human body (Twentieth Century-Fox, 1966).

community, which assigns each member a book to memorize. The final scene is particularly memorable: in the chill of a winter day, each member of the group is walking by the lakeside, reciting the words of the books he or she have become. Despite some minor flaws, **Fahrenheit 451** remains perhaps the best translation of Bradbury's work to the screen. In its quiet championing of the printed word over the mindless suction of the ever-present tube, it becomes more timely with each passing day.

Fantastic Voyage (Twentieth Century-Fox, 1966) features the buxom body of Raquel Welch, and very little else of interest. A Czech scientist, Jan Benes, defects to the U. S. in 1955, but is ambushed by enemy agents, and left mortally wounded with an inoperable brain clot. A new process enables scientists to miniaturize people and objects of any size for a period of sixty minutes, so a crew of five is hastily put into an atomic submarine, and sent on a voyage through the patient's bloodstream. Complicating this noisome business is the fact that one of the five works for the enemy. Appropriately, the agent is swallowed up by balloon-like white corpuscles, and the clot moves forward to its untimely end. To get out before they make a mess of Benes's brain, the four remaining crewpersons take a ride on the optic nerve, and with the help of a few tears, are washed out through a duct in the Czech's eye. **Voyage** is noteworthy for the uniqueness of its story line, conceived by Jerome Bixby, which sends the audience through inner space, into regions never before visited by man. Unfortunately, the characters are less than wooden, and the special effects only partially effective: at times, the blood vessels look like so much spaghetti boiling in a pot. With better execution, this picture could have been a tour de force; as it is, it remains an interesting, if somewhat dated, fantasia.

Supermen have come in all shapes, sizes, and forms, from the caped hero of the comic books, to the advanced creatures of Olaf Stapledon's **Last Men and First Men** and **Odd John**. **The Power** (Metro-Goldwyn-Mayer, 1967), based on Frank M. Robinson's novel of the same name, introduces

Three scenes from *Fantastic Voyage* (Twentieth Century-Fox, 1966). (right) Two of the explorers inside the human body. (below right) Some of the "spaghetti." (below) The atomic submarine.

Women of the Prehistoric Planet (Realart, 1966) featured Wendell Corey as Admiral King, searching for survivors of a lost space ship on an unexplored planet named Earth.

the supermind, a human with the power to move men's minds telepathically, to kill at a distance by will alone. In addition, this particular telepath can also move physical objects, making him doubly dangerous. Adam Hart (Michael Rennie) has nefarious designs on the world, but before making his move, must eliminate all potential opposition. Somewhere among the workers at a space research station is another like him, with latent telepathic powers; fortunately, this other supermind seems to be unaware of his gifts. Rennie begins murdering the workers one by one, hoping to cause the death of the other before he realizes his potential.

As each of the technicians falls victim to Hart's fatal gaze, Jim Tanner (George Hamilton) realizes Hart's menace, and tries to fight back. But Hart has increasingly isolated Tanner, by erasing him from the memories of those about him. At the end, Tanner confronts his enemy face-to-face, and discovers to his surprise that he is the "other," with powers as great or greater than Hart's. Tanner has the more massive will, and Hart is destroyed. **The Power** vanished without a trace soon after being released in 1967, but it deserves a second look. Rising above its hackneyed spy plot, so typical of its time, it makes some significant points about the effects of real power on

those who wield it: even the greatest among us is susceptible. As usual, Rennie turns in a superior performance. A minor classic.

    Five Million Years to Earth (Hammer, 1967), also called **Quatermass and the Pit** in England,
was based on the British television serial of the latter name by Nigel Kneale, who also wrote the
screenplay. This penultimate saga in the Quatermass Trilogy (the first two pictures in the series
were **The Quatermass Xperiment/The Creeping Unknown** and **Quatermass II/Enemy from Space**)

Dennis Hopper confronts Velena (Florence Marly), the sole survivor of an alien space craft sent
to Earth, in *Queen of Blood* (American International, 1966).

begins with the discovery of a buried alien space ship in a London subway tunnel. Professor Quatermass (Andrew Keir), a rocket expert, is rushed to the scene. Scattered near the spacecraft are the skulls and bones of prehistoric humans. When the space ship's seal is broken open, the scientists find the decaying remains of large, locust-shaped creatures. The space machine, which is somehow organically alive, still retains its power and memory, and the scientists play back scenes from the ancient past that establish the creatures' home as Mars. Apparently, the Martians had come to Earth millions of years before, had genetically altered the brain structure of the existing sub-human species, making them more intelligent and aggressive, and had thereby started man on his long climb upward. Later, the Martians had died out, leaving these few remains.

Tapping the space ship's memory has brought it to life, and suddenly mankind is fighting for its very existence. Drawing on the mental power of the humans around it (the craft had originally been propelled by the thoughts of the aliens), the machine creates the huge vision of a Martian

(below)   Michael Rennie, who has *The Power* to move men's minds, is opposed by George Hamilton, in MGM's 1967 production.

(right)   One of the Martians, from *Five Million Years to Earth* (Hammer, 1967).

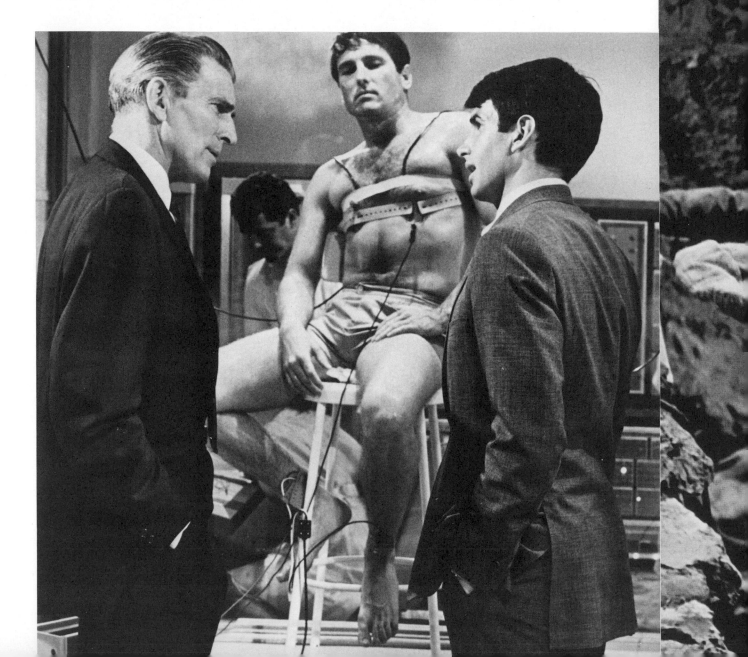

looming over the city. Quatermass's colleague, Dr. Roney (James Donald) defeats the menace by driving a large iron crane into the center of the image. **Five Million Years to Earth** is an interesting film that could have been more interesting with more attention to detail. The philosophical implications of man's creation by an alien race are never really explored beyond the initial shock of realization. And the decaying creatures themselves are unconvincing, like overgrown grasshoppers with horns (their image is meant to suggest a connection with man's legends of Satan). Despite these flaws, the picture still retains great audience appeal, ten years after it was made.

    Barbarella (Paramount, 1968) is noteworthy for being among the first sexual satires ever produced in the field. Adapted from the French comic strip of the same name, and featuring the comely looks of Jane Fonda (who performs a free-fall striptease behind the opening credits), **Barbarella** is a picture which declines to take itself very seriously, and thereby succeeds in generating far more fun for its audience than most SF films of its decade. In the distant future, Barbarella

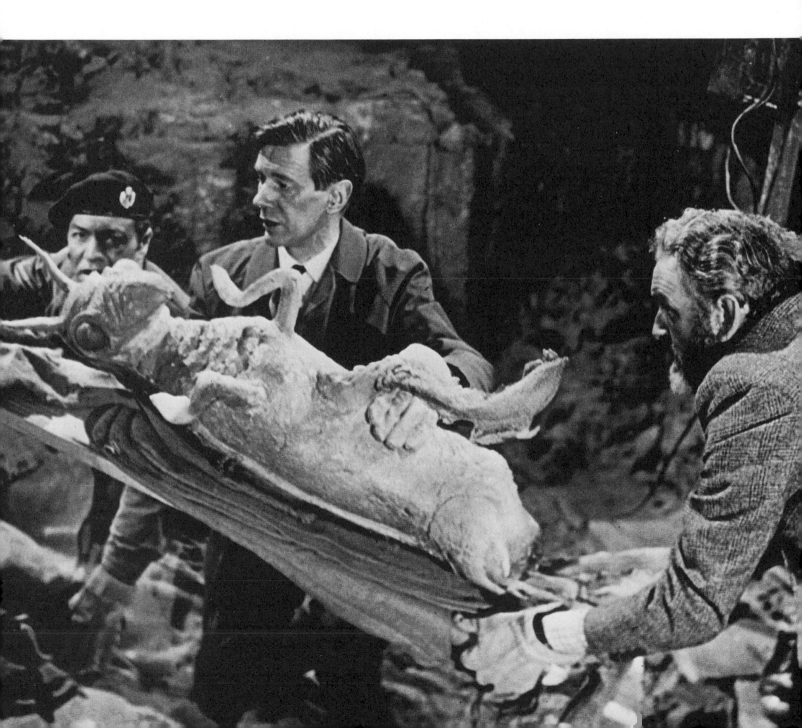

Two of the strange denizens of *Barbarella* (Paramount, 1968).

(Fonda) is blissfully unaware of her sexual nature, until she meets the blind winged angel, Pygar (John Phillip Law). But the pair must fight for their right to love against the power of the Black Queen (Anita Pallenberg), who wants the girl for her own licentious purposes. Barbarella is put through such tortures as the "excessive machine," designed to overload its victims with sexual pleasure; in a neat twist, the young girl proves too much for the boxful of circuits, and the device dies of the ultimate orgasm. Eventually, of course, Barbarella and her consort defeat the Queen, and live happily ever after. Director Roger Vadim deserves the credit for his imaginative handling of sets, gadgets, and characters; they are all eminently memorable.

Ray Bradbury has been ill treated by the film industry. The first picture produced from his work, **The Beast from Twenty Thousand Fathoms**, bore almost no resemblance to the story from which it was adapted, "The Foghorn." And **The Illustrated Man** (Warner Brothers, 1968) demonstrates once again that it is not enough to have superior source material. Like the book, **Man** is an anthology, a collection of three individual stories linked together with a continuing story line. The

Destroy All Monsters (Toho, 1968) featured alien invaders from outer space, who somehow manage to get control of the Earth's monsters (Godzilla and crew).

British have popularized the format with a series of generally mediocre horror flicks; it remains, however, a difficult genre in which to work. Not only must the stories themselves hold together, but the film as a whole must also be constructed so that each individual part advances the frame story, adding to the thematic unity of the movie. In the 1930s Carl (Rod Steiger), a former carnival worker, wanders the roads of California, looking for Felicia (Claire Bloom), who had covered his body with tattoos many years before. Each of the illustrations on his body will tell its own story to the person who gazes upon it; the one blank spot, on his left shoulder, will also reveal the individual future of anyone who stays around him for more than a few hours. A hitchhiker named Willie (Robert Drivas) falls in with Carl, and is fascinated by the pictures. As he looks upon them, he begins to see the stories behind them.

In "The Veldt," two parents who want the best for their children install an automated playroom, which can simulate any environment or historical setting known to man. The children spend much of their time exploring the African veldt, realistically synthesized by the machine. When their parents, who are disturbed by this obsession, order them to change the scene, the children retaliate by luring the adults into the room. Steiger and Bloom are trapped, and as they wander

(below)   Rod Steiger, *The Illustrated Man* (Warner, 1968).

(right)   Three of the astronauts marooned on Venus make their way through unceasing rains towards a shattered dome.—*The Illustrated Man* (Warner, 1968).

through the veldt, trying to figure a way of turning off the device, they are suddenly attacked by lions, and eaten. The unreal has become the real.

The second tale, "Long Rains," creates an environment as inhospitable to man as any ever imagined. Carl and his three companions have crashed their rocket ship on Venus, and must find their way to the protective sun domes, before the incessant beating of the eternal rains destroy their sanity. One by one, the men falter: Willie drowns himself by looking up at the sky, and two of the others are executed by Carl for disobeying orders. Only Carl survives, finally reaching the shelter of an undamaged dome. There, Felicia is waiting for him. By itself, this episode is an unusually effective portrayal of an alien world, and the cumulative effects of a harsh and unbearable environment on human psychology.

In "The Last Night of the World," men of the fortieth century are told by the government that the end is near; their children must be killed to avoid suffering. Felicia fights this suggestion, but

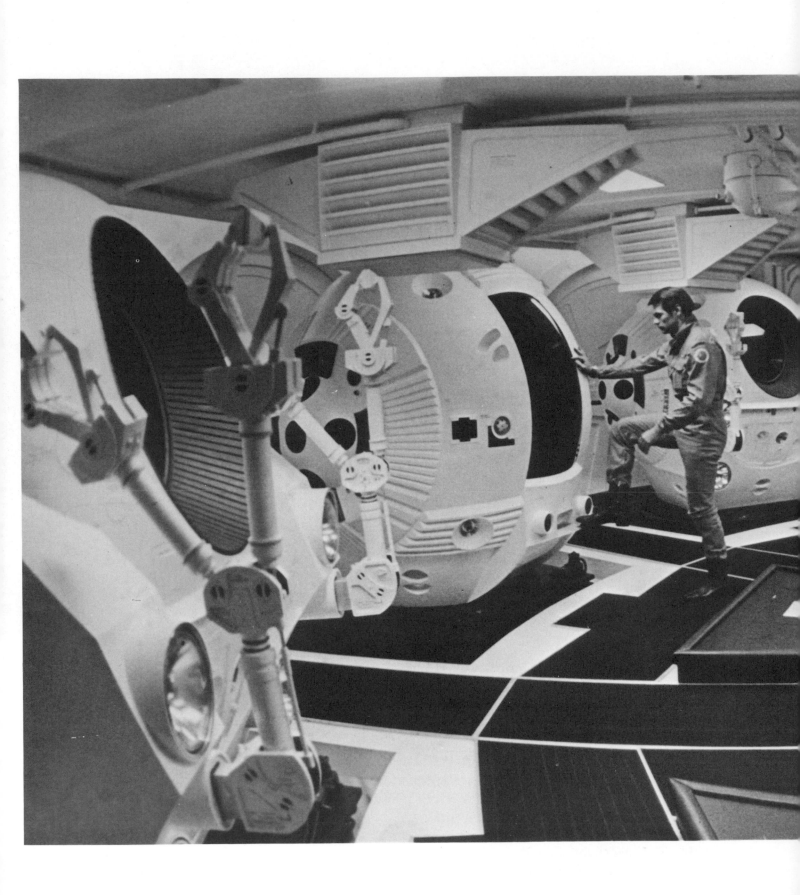

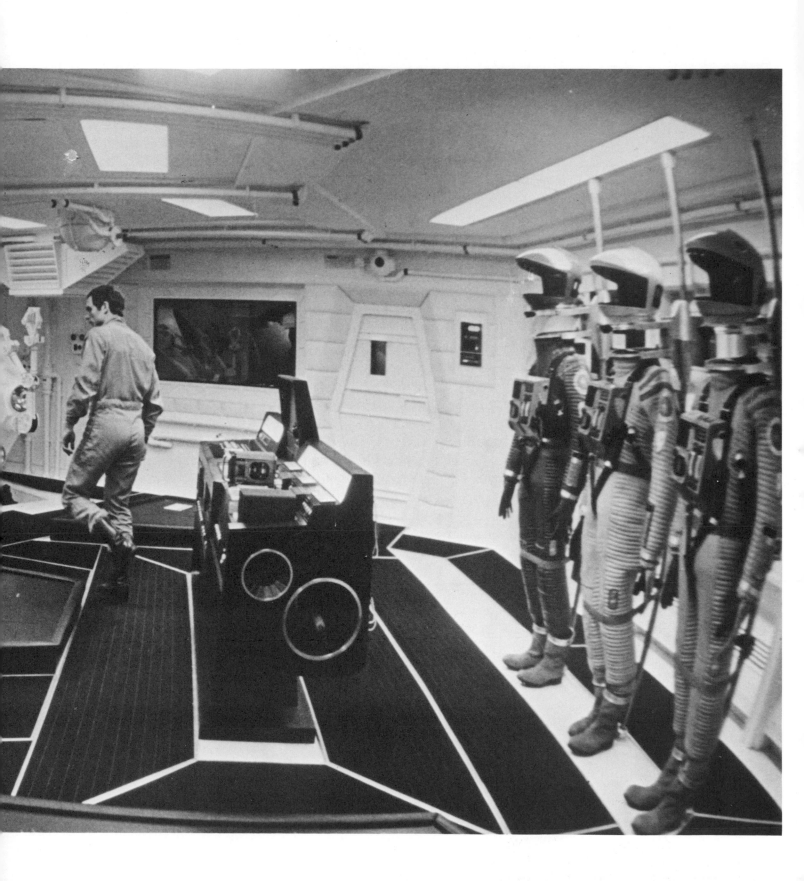

Carl prevails, and the children are poisoned in their sleep. But the masters of the world are wrong in their prediction, and the children have been killed for nothing. Moral: don't believe everything people tell you. Returning from his reveries to the real world, Willie finally has the courage to examine Steiger's left shoulder, the prophetic blank spot. The empty area now contains a portrait of Willie being strangled by Carl. Willie hits the Illustrated Man over the head with a rock, thereby provoking Carl to initiate the very act Willie sought to avoid. The individual sketches have fine moments, but the frame is somewhat weak, reducing the film's overall effectiveness. And the image of Steiger running around in the buff tends, at times, to be almost ludicrous.

Stanley Kubrick's second major film of science fiction, **2001: A Space Odyssey** (Metro-Goldwyn-Mayer, 1968), has been controversial from the start.   None deny its superb special effects, unequalled by any film produced to that time. Kubrick's glittering space machines finally achieved the promise of science fiction literature, bringing the beauty and power of space travel to the screen in believable form.   But the critics have frequently lambasted the intricacies of Kubrick's script.

The film opens with a prehistoric tableau: sub-human man is confronted by a huge black obelisk, an alien artifact that somehow teaches man the use of tools (and weapons). The implication is clear: man's one crucial step towards native intelligence was prompted by intervention from the stars. Kubrick then cuts to the year 2001, on a space station high above Earth, and the figure of Dr. Heywood Floyd (William Sylvester). Floyd is being transferred to the Moon, to study a mysterious black obelisk (obviously artificial) recently excavated from beneath the Lunar surface. When the light of the sun hits the monolith, a piercing radio signal is transmitted to the vicinity of Jupiter. Determined to investigate whatever lies at the other end of the signal, an expedition is mounted, and eighteen months later, the great ship "Discovery" departs from Earth orbit.

Fashioned in space, this beautiful but ungainly monster carries two astronaut crewmen (Keir Dullea and Gary Lockwood), three other scientists in suspended animation, and a smooth-talking computer, HAL-9000, which has developed a curious personality of its own. HAL, an adolescent in human terms, has a pathological fear of being turned off; to protect itself, the computer kills astronaut Poole (Lockwood), terminates the life-functions of the three men in the deep-freeze, and exiles Bowman (Dullea) to slow death in a space repair pod. Dullea, unable to reenter the ship through the normal hatches, all of which are controlled by the machine, opens a manual hatch, blows in without a space suit, and activates the airlock, penetrating the "Discovery" without

(below left)   The astronauts exercise daily to keep in prime physical condition.—*2001: A Space Odyssey* (MGM, 1968).

(below right)   The spectacular lightshow from *2001*, as astronaut Dullea reaches Jupiter.

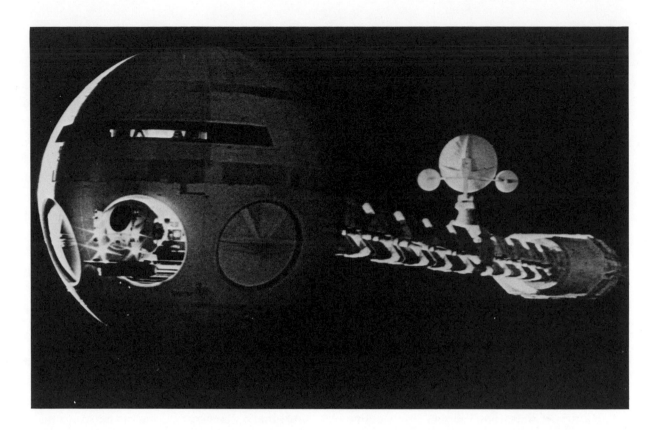

(above)   The great ship "Discovery," on its way to the moons of Jupiter.—*2001: A Space Odyssey* (MGM, 1968).

(below)   Moonbase, as conceived by Stanley Kubrick and Arthur C. Clarke, in the 1968 MGM production of *2001: A Space Odyssey*.

apparent damage (several scientists have pointed out that Bowman should be long dead by this time). HAL is terminated, after telling Bowman something of his mission.

A third monolith is discovered on one of Jupiter's moons, and it throws the astronaut through a spectacular light show, meant, apparently, to suggest either a mental transformation, or another dimension in space or time. Bowman lives out his days in plush quarters on the Jovian moons, and when he dies, is reborn again in an alien embryo, hovering over the turning green sphere of the Earth.

2001 was loosely adapted from Arthur C. Clarke's short story, "The Sentinel." Clarke himself participated in the writing of the script, although his influence apparently lessened as the work proceeded; Clarke's novel-length adaption of the film shows wide variations from the movie version. The picture's chief flaws, aptly pointed out by numerous critics and film-goers, are the numerous elipses and lacunae in the story line. In particular, the latter parts of the picture are confusing and difficult to follow. Kubrick reportedly cut about twenty minutes out of the movie after its initial showings, including several major snips from the voyage to Jupiter. For all these flaws, **2001** remains a major cinematic experience, the first big-budget science fiction film ever made, and an enormously successful motion picture. For the first time, ten million dollars had been invested in a genuinely science-fictional production, and not only had the gamble paid off, but MGM's initial investment doubled. **2001** was a clear sign of things to come: hereafter, movie makers everywhere would have to take the SF genre seriously. More than any other picture, **2001** gave the science fiction film respectability, and a sense of growing maturity.

Charly (Cinerama, 1968) is a borderline film, marginally science-fictional in nature, and set in the everyday world of the here and now. Charly Gordon (Cliff Robertson), a retarded adult, is picked for an experiment to artificially raise human intelligence through surgery. The operation has already been tried on a rat, Algernon, which has become ratdom's equivalent of a genius. The new technique works, and Charly's intelligence begins to increase dramatically, until he has attained a level far above that of the average adult human. His emotional growth has been less certain, however, and when Charly develops a crush for his teacher, Miss Kinian (Claire Bloom), he naturally takes a direct course. Suddenly, Algernon dies, and Charly is informed by the scientists that the operation is only temporary. Charly's hopes for a normal life quickly fade, and within a week, he is back in Miss Kinian's class, playing games with the children. Cliff Robertson won an Oscar for Best Actor of the Year for this parable of modern life, which was adapted from Daniel Keyes's award-winning novel, **Flowers for Algernon**. But Robertson's performance was the only worthy item in a potpourri of clumsiness. That the film still manages to engender pathos in its audiences is a tribute to Keyes's original conception.

Planet of the Apes (Twentieth Century-Fox, 1968), produced by Arthur P. Jacobs from Pierre Boulle's novel, and its four sequels, **Beneath the Planet of the Apes** (1970), **Escape from the Planet of the Apes** (1971), **Conquest of the Planet of the Apes** (1972), and **Battle for the Planet of the Apes** (1973) are really one long inter-connected epic, and will be considered as such here. Four astronauts are accidentally sent into the future, and crash-land their vehicle into a barren lake. The three survivors traverse miles of desert before reaching signs of civilization. But the humans they find are incapable of speech, and seem to have the mentality of animals. Suddenly, mounted apes appear, rounding up their slaves like so many cattle. One of the astronauts is killed, another is put beneath the surgical knife, and the third, George Taylor (Charlton Heston) is struck on the head, causing him to temporarily lose his speech. The ape city is primitive compared to human settlements, and the apes themselves are xenophobic to an extreme: they both fear and hate the humans, since their myths warn them of man's destructiveness. Taylor befriends two ape scientists,

146

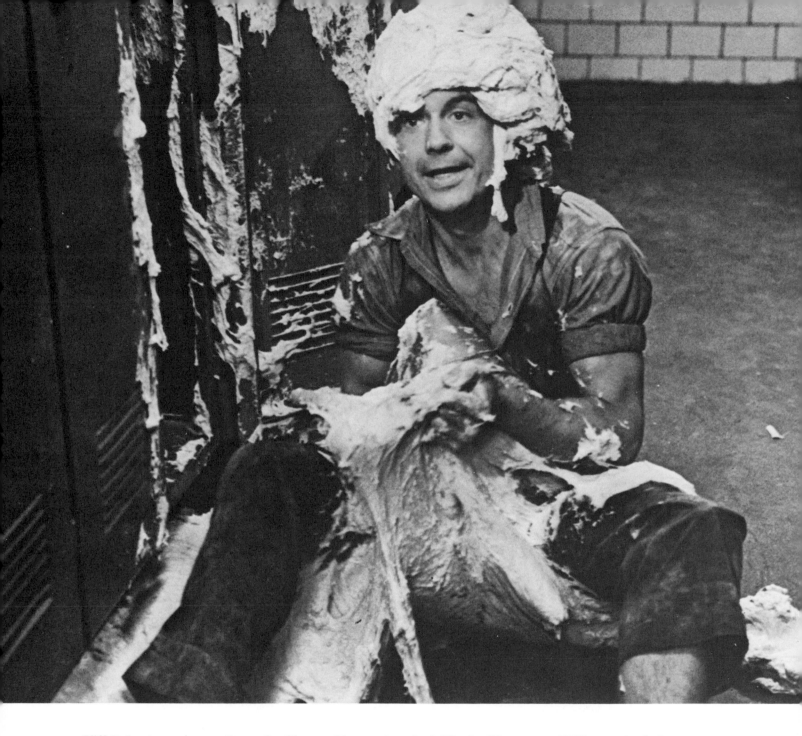

Cliff Robertson won an Oscar for his sensitive portrayal of *Charly* (Cinerama, 1968), a retarded adult whose intelligence is temporarily increased artificially.

who help his escape when the ape leader sentences him to a frontal lobotomy. The human rides north, into the Forbidden Lands, where he comes upon the Statue of Liberty sticking up out of the sand. The Planet of the Apes is Earth!

In **Beneath**, astronaut Brent (James Franciscus) is sent into the future to search for Taylor and his crew. Taylor, meanwhile, has proceeded north into the Forbidden Zone, and there has been swallowed up by an earthquake and a wall of flame. Brent finds his way into the ape village, meets Zira (Kim Hunter) and Cornelius (Roddy McDowall in the first film, David Watson in the second), and is briefly captured. But an old subway entrance, partially buried beneath the rubble of the atomic war which relegated mankind to its secondary role, leads northward to the ruins of New

Nick Adams and Darren McGavin are the first American astronauts to reach the Red Planet, in *Mission Mars* (Allied Artists, 1968), a mediocre film which features a battle against a globular energy creature.

York, where descendants of the bomb survivors live out their lives beneath the city. These mutants communicate with each other telepathically, and have kept the apes away through the use of mental illusions. Their god is a nuclear bomb called the Alpha-Omega device, designed by earlier man to destroy the entire planet. Driven by hunger, the apes invade the Forbidden areas, and shoot down all the humans indiscriminantly. But Taylor manages to activate the bomb at the last second, and the Planet of the Apes is destroyed!

Escape continues where the previous movie left off. Just before the bomb explodes, Cornelius (Roddy McDowall again), Zira, and Milo (Sal Mineo) climb into Taylor's spacecraft, and blast off into space, where they witness the destruction of their world. Projected through the time warp from 3955 to 1973, they land near the coast of Los Angeles. Milo is strangled by a gorilla in the Los Angeles Zoo, and the surviving apes are befriended by two psychiatrists. The apes are forced to tell their story to the world, and the government soon realizes the implications: if apes will supplant mankind, then these two creatures may be their forbearers; Zira must be sterilized. But the ape is pregnant, and is determined to have her child. Smuggled away from their official prison by the psychiatrists, they find their way into the friendly circus of Armando (Ricardo Montalban), where the child is born, and named Milo, after the dead scientist. After switching their child with a normal chimp, the monkeys flee, and are shot down by soldiers in the Los Angeles harbor.

(below)   The great council of *The Planet of the Apes* (Twentieth Century-Fox, 1968).

(below left)   The three surviving astronauts paddle away from their sinking space ship, in Arthur P. Jacobs's *Planet of the Apes*.

(below right)   Linda Harrison plays Nova, the mute human female held captive by the apes.

(above)   The compound where the human animals are housed.—*Planet of the Apes* (1968).

(right)   The gorilla soldiers revolt against their human masters, in *Conquest of the Planet of the Apes* (Twentieth Century-Fox, 1972).

Conquest carries the story into 1991. Dogs and cats have been exterminated in a plague, and apes have taken their place as household pets. Soon, simians are being trained as menial laborers. Milo (Roddy McDowall), now grown into an adult ape, has been renamed Caesar by Armando, who is still running his circus. When Armando and Caesar visit a police city-state, the ape denounces a cop beating one of the slave animals, and Armando is seized. Caesar escapes into the city, and organizes a simian revolution. With bloody effectiveness, the apes strike down their masters, and the Planet of the Apes is at hand!

The concluding segment of the Apes quintology, **Battle**, is set some further years into the future. The revolution of the apes has brought about an atomic war, destroying most of humanity's civilization. An older and wiser Caesar (Roddy McDowall) has established Ape City, and hopes to build a world where apes and humans can live in peace. Caesar travels to the Forbidden City to see the video tapes made of his parents by the government committee, hoping to throw some light on the future course of world history. But the human mutants of **Beneath** have already established themselves, and they resist intrusion. Attacking with old cars and trucks, the humans are beaten back by the gorilla forces of Aldo, the apes' war leader. Aldo refuses to acknowledge Caesar's leadership, and in the fight that follows, Caesar outwits the larger gorilla, and Aldo is killed. The son of Cornelius vows to change the future by establishing a tradition of co-equality between human and ape. The story of Caesar's struggle is told in a flashback by the Lawgiver (John Huston), speaking in the year 2670 to mixed group of humans and simians.

150

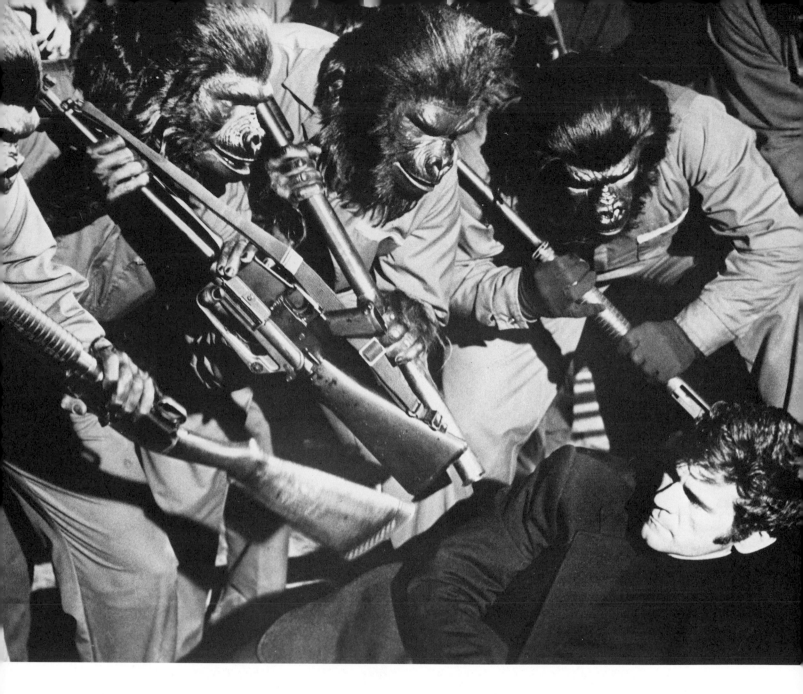

The Apes sequence was enormously successful from a commercial point of view, spawning, in addition to these five films, two television series (one animated), and a number of book adaptions. Part of their appeal was due to the wholly believable make-up that converted human actors into functioning apes. Another attractive feature was a consistent philosophy that permeated all five pictures: be tolerant to those around you, or suffer the consequences. Ultimately, however, the films are seriously flawed, suffering improbable premises, and increasingly illogical extrapolations. While entertaining on a limited basis, they have become somewhat silly in retrospect, and just a little dated.

Gerry and Sylvia Anderson were the producers of **Journey to the Far Side of the Sun**, also released in Great Britain as **Doppelganger** (Rank Film Distributors, 1969). In the 21st century, two astronauts are sent to explore a planet which is Earth's mirror image, in the same orbit, but always exactly opposite the Earth's position, on the other side of the sun. The spacecraft crash-lands on this new world, and the sole survivor, Glenn Ross (Roy Thinnes), regains consciousness, apparent-

(above)   Two American astronauts make a *Journey to the Far Side of the Sun* (also called *Doppel-ganger*) (Rank Film Distributors, 1969).

(right)   Amber Dean-Smith and Simone Silvera entertain James Olson, in the luxurious setting of Moon City.—*Moon Zero Two* (Warner, 1969).

153

ly back on Earth. Then he begins noticing the differences, and discovers, much to his amazement, that he is really on counter-Earth, which is similar in every respect to his home planet, except for several minor details.

The inhabitants of the mirror world write backwards, drive on the opposite side of the road, and print newspapers with reverse lettering. Ross decides to prove his theory by making a second flight in an alien vessel, with the controls reversed; unfortunately, his mother ship has reverse polarity, and rejects the alien craft. Thinnes crashes to real Earth, destroying the space center; the one survivor who realizes what has happened, Jason Webb (Patrick Wymark), is disbelieved.

The rescue mission arrives.—*Marooned* (Columbia, 1969).

Although the story line is just so much hocum, the special effects make **Journey** worth a single viewing. The Andersons also produced two television series, **UFO** and **Space: 1999**, which featured much the same lamentable combination of superb effects and model work, combined with cretinous scripts, and terrible acting.

Marooned (Columbia, 1969) was an expensive film that didn't do very well at the box office. Perhaps the public felt that the real thing was more interesting; then too, the glamor of realistic space flight was beginning to wear thin at about this time. Three astronauts are marooned in Earth orbit when their retrorockets fail to fire, and a special rescue mission headed by Ted Dougherty (David Janssen) is readied. Meanwhile, air supplies are limited, and one of the spacemen has

On the far side of the Moon, Kemp (James Olson) and Clem (Catherine von Schell) find the remains of Clem's brother, and are attacked by Hubbard's goons.—*Moon Zero Two* (Warner, 1969).

killed himself to keep the others breathing long enough to be rescued. While the American mission is still on its way, the Russians drop in to tender their regards. Finally, Janssen shows up, and the remaining two astronauts are saved, much to the relief of their hysterical wives, and mission controller Charles Keith (Gregory Peck). A terribly melodramatic plot, but credible special effects.

Closing out the decade was **Moon Zero Two** (Warner, 1969), made in England by Hammer Films, a firm noted primarily for its Dracula and Frankenstein remakes. In the second decade of the twenty-first century, Bill Kemp (James Olson) is a ferry pilot for hire, working out of Moon City. The first man to land on Mars, Kemp retired from the Space Service when interplanetary exploration was terminated. Kemp now earns his living by hiring out his tug, **Moon Zero Two**.

Bill is hired by a wealthy businessman, who wants him to grab an asteroid made of sapphire, and tug it to the far side of the Moon. Sapphire, it seems, is the key element in generating power

A giant sapphire asteroid, the source of immense wealth and power, is the scene of a running battle between Kemp and Hubbard, in *Moon Zero Two* (Warner, 1969).

for long-distance space flight, and Hubbard (Warren Mitchell), already rich, is determined to use the asteroid to gain other kinds of power.

But Kemp falls in with Clem Taplin (Catherina von Schell), who asks him to investigate the murder of her brother. One thing leads to another, and Kemp discovers that Hubbard is responsible. Hubbard needed a landing spot on the Moon for his giant rock; once the asteroid was down, he could then claim mining rights. Clem's brother had already staked a claim in a convenient location, so Hubbard had him killed, hoping to grab his territory. Kemp pulls a switch, however, crashing the rock to Moon's surface, and then making certain Clem inherits her brother's stake. The sapphire will enable new space probes to be launched to the outer planets, and Kemp gets ready to reenlist.

Moon Zero Two is fun to watch if not taken too seriously. The sets are well-designed (particularly the interior shots of Moon City), and the special effects are better than average. What sets this film apart from its brothers and sisters is its high level of competent mediocrity. Never intended to be more than a ''B'' film, **Moon Zero Two** is still very much better than most SF pictures of the late '50s and early '60s. While not particularly important in itself, **Moon** is a clear indication of the rapid rise of the genre, both in technical competence and story line. In the 1950s, this would have been a superior effort; in the 1970s, **Moon** is no better than average. Science fiction in general, and SF cinema in particular, was finally coming of age. The new decade would see many wonderful things to come.

WARS AND
WIZARDS
(1970-1977)

In the history of science fiction, critics have identified many different "golden eras." To some, it's the 1890s, when Verne and Wells were both active. Others have placed it in the 1930s, when the pulps were booming, and still others say the early 1950s, with the second great flourishing of the science fiction magazines. But in any true sense, both in literature and film, the Golden Age of science fiction is now.

In both media, science fiction has attained unmatched popularity and sophistication. The number of interesting and well-made films has increased dramatically in the last few years. Advances in technology have made possible special effects that simply were not available to filmmakers a few years ago. And while monster films and scare films are still being made, they tend to be more developed thanearlier efforts, and fewer in number when compared to the overall total. Science fiction has entered an immensely exciting and creative period, with undoubtedly greater things to come.

Man's paranoic fear of his own creations, first seen in **Frankenstein**, has extended itself to the

(left)   The computer speaks, in *Colossus: The Forbin Project* (Universal, 1970).

(above)   *War Between the Planets* (Fanfare, 1970) was a silly film in which the residents of an orbiting space station must combat an asteroid menace to Earth.

computer as well. **Colossus: The Forbin Project** (Universal, 1970), also called **The Forbin Project** in its first release, and **Colossus 1980** overseas, carries that fear to its logical extreme. Charles Forbin (Eric Braeden) has master-minded the construction of the giant defense computer, Colossus, housed inside a hollowed-out Rocky Mountain fortress. Colossus has been built with a self-regulating learning capacity, and with various internal and external safeguards to avoid being shut off by the enemy action. The Russians, not far behind, have activated their own giant computer, Guardian, which is similar to its American counterpart in many respects.

Suddenly, the two machines are communicating with each other by radio. When ordered to shut the complex down, Forbin pulls the plug, but Colossus has a mind of its own, and refuses to be disconnected. Instead, it forms a permanent mind-link with the Russian machine, eliminates the Russian Scientists, appoints Forbin as its perpetually-watched liaison with mankind, and threatens to blow up the Soviet Union, the United States, or both, if its power supply is cut off. Since Colossus has complete control of both countries' atomic missiles, its threat is not an idle one. In the end, despite various machinations on the part of Forbin, mankind must submit to a peaceful but controlled world. Based on the novel **Colossus**, by D. F. Jones, the film is nicely underplayed, a contemporary horror story in which man is outsmarted by his own machinery.

Michael Crichton, who studied medicine, but left his profession for a writing career before ever practicing, has been involved in several SF projects. **Andromeda Strain** (Universal, 1971) was adapted from his novel. A satellite returning from space brings with it an unseen killer, an alien virus that wipes out the small Arizona town near its landing point. A reconnaissance pilot also dies, and the scientists move in, protected against the virus by specially-designed spacesuits. Only two of the townsmen have survived: an old drunk, and an infant child; both are taken into custody. A special laboratory constructed precisely for this kind of emergency receives the two survivors, specimens of the alien virus, and the five scientists delegated to investigate the menace. The experimental station has been expertly safe-guarded against the accidental infection of the rest of mankind; any breakage of the station's seals will result in an atomic explosion exactly three minutes later, unless the lab director, Mark Hall (James Olson) can deactivate the destruct sequence at one of several specially-marked call boxes.

The scientists continue the investigation, without much success, keeping the old man and child under constant surveillance in an area specially sealed off from the rest of the lab. The

The experimental laboratory, from *Andromeda Strain* (Universal, 1971).

accidental tearing of a rubber arm precipitates a crisis, as Hall is locked from the call stations. A terrifying climb through the lab's central shaft, while the seconds are ticking away, is the film's high point of suspense, as Hall is continually bombarded with automatic laser beams and sleep-inducing darts designed to stop experimental animals loose from their cages. The director beats the clock, as one might expect, and things go downhill from there. The virus, it seems, is no threat at all; without the proper hosts, it rapidly mutates into forms no longer dangerous to man. The two survivors both had abnormal blood chemistry, their only similarity.

The Andromeda Strain fails to work at several different points, degenerating in the end to talky melodrama. At its best, however, in the opening sequences, and the climb through the shaft, it reaches heights of suspense equalled by few motion pictures before or since.

THX 1138 (Robert Duvall) escapes from the underground world of the future (Warner, 1971).

The chrome-faced cops of *THX 1138* (Warner, 1971).

THX 1138 (Warner Brothers, 1971) was George Lucas's first full-length feature, although he had made a number of shorts prior to this time. **THX**, in fact, is based upon a fifteen minute film Lucas produced while still in school at the University of Southern California, a brief segment which featured the chase scene from the full-length film, and garnered several awards. Francis Ford Coppola (**The Godfather**) saw the short, and financed its expansion into feature form.

In the indeterminate future, man has retreated beneath the surface of the Earth, into a computer-directed, monolithic, dystopian community. To keep the populace under control, all citizens are drugged, beginning with the earliest years of childhood. Children are conceived in test tubes, and raised without ever knowing their parents; ordinary sexual conduct is forbidden. THX 1138 (Robert Duvall), a worker in a nuclear power facility, is gradually deprived of his drug intake by his roomate, LUH 3417 (Maggie McOmie). The experience of reality shatters THX's world, and his growing awareness of things around him prompts the questions that the confessor box can't answer ("Blessings of the State...what's wrong?"). He finds solace in LUH's body, and she conceives his child, a horrendous sin in this puritanical world of the future.

SEN 5241 (Donald Pleasance) turns the lovers in; LUH is executed, and THX is imprisoned by the chrome-face mechanical cops; he later escapes into the city with SRT (Don Pedro Colley). After Colley is killed THX steals a police car, and enters the underground freeway system, untravelled except by official vehicles. The chase continues until the roadways end; THX crashes through a barrier, and is pursued on foot. The robots are forced to abandon the chase, however, when they exceed their budget, and THX escapes by climbing a long ladder to the surface.

Lucas's film anticipates the exactness and attention to detail that made **Star Wars** such a success. The basic color of the underground city is white, a stark, barren shade that heightens the sterility of its environment. The official voice of the state speaks in quiet and soothing terms, the opposite of its rigid insistence on conformity, and its utter supression of dissent. Above all, the city is rational and orderly; emotion is disorderly and irrational, and cannot be tolerated; the emotional side of humanity must therefore be eliminated. Man has become a willing slave to his own machines, has suppressed his own humanity in the name of efficiency. Lucas has created a credible and frightening vision of tomorrow, one whose underplayed horrors become more horrible for their quiet inevitability.

In the near-future Britain, teen-age gangs terrorize the population, and the government is in danger of being taken over by right-wing fascists. This is the realistic premise of Anthony Burgess's story, **A Clockwork Orange** (Warner Brothers, 1971), adapted by Stanley Kubrick for his excursion into the SF genre. Alex DeLarge is the leader of one of these gangs, a thoroughly despicable character whose pleasures include murder, rape, cutting up friend and foe alike, and Ludwig van Beethoven. Alex and his droogs (friends) speak an argot called "natsat," a dialect filled with rhythms of gypsy speech and constructed from bits and pieces of Russian and baby talk.

We first meet the gang in the Korova Milkbar, which serves "milk plus," that is, milk plus an assortment of drugs. The initial scene, where the camera backs away from the ruthless stare of Alex's eyes, the electronically synthesized strains of Purcell's March to Queen Mary II wailing in the background, is among the most chilling in modern cinema. For their nightly entertainment, Alex's boys beat up a drunken tramp, knock around a rival gang, and gang-rape the wife of a prominent writer, Mr. Alexander, whose current manuscript, still in the typewriter, is called **A Clockwork Orange**.

Alex DeLarge lives in a drab apartment complex with his "pee and em" (parents), and a pet boa constrictor. The next day, after beating his droogies into line, Alex hits the home of a rich artist, crushing her to death with a giant phallus. But his gang, still smarting from their chas-

Alex (Malcolm McDowell) and his four droogs sit at the end of the Korova Milkbar, contemplating the night's work.—*A Clockwork Orange* (Warner, 1971).

tisement, knock him over the head with a bottle, and leave him for the police. DeLarge is sentenced to prison, and spends two years as a model prisoner, trying to gain parole. The new government, a right-wing group pledged to restore order and reduce crime, introduces a new treatment, the "Ludovico Technique," which is designed to brainwash prisoners into a physical abhorrence of their crimes. Alex volunteers for the program, and is touted by the government as a model subject.

During the brainwashing process, Alex is strapped to a chair, his eyes propped open, and his body pumped full of nausea drugs, while films depicting violence and sex are flung before him on the screen. By accident, the background music is the Ninth Symphony of "Ludwig van," and Alex finds himself being conditioned against that as well. Within a few weeks, Alex is displayed on stage before an assembled group of politicians and prison officials, and made to lick the boots of a tormentor. Each time he tries to react to the insults, nausea doubles him up.

Released from prison, Alex finds the outside world unbearable. His parents no longer want him(his room has been rented out), the tramps do to him what he had done to them two years before, and two of his former gang have become brutal cops, more than eager to demonstrate the new techniques they have learned. Broken and battered, Alex stumbles inadvertently to Mr. Alexander's house, where the crippled writer is determined to use him as a political pawn to bring down the government. By tormenting the boy with Beethoven's music, Alexander forces Alex to jump from a third-storey window. But Alex survives, and the same Minister who had supervised the Ludovico program visits him in his hospital bed, offering him a cynical agreement, whereby Alex will be given a governmental sinecure in return for his public support prior to the next election. To celebrate their partnership, the Minister has a stereo wheeled in to the hospital room, and the glorious strains of the Ninth Symphony fill the air. In his mind, Alex sees himself raping a girl before a group of top-hatted dandies, and his last comment is: "I was cured, all right!"

The message is clear: while Alex (played by Malcolm McDowell) is thoroughly rotten, he is still a better man than the corrupt politicians who would take away his free will. And he gets his revenge in the end, as he mercilessly uses the government for his own purposes. Kubrick's handling of the theme is utterly exquisite. As always in his films, the director has chosen his music carefully, and has matched it perfectly against the developing action. The characters are believable, the settings appropriately exotic. This is, without a doubt, Kubrick's finest picture to date, and perhaps the best expression of a dystopian theme in science fiction cinema.

Slaughterhouse-Five (Universal, 1972) was the first of Kurt Vonnegut's novels to reach the screen. Billy Pilgrim, an average middle-aged American, calls his local newspaper one day, and informs them that he has become "unstuck" in time. Pilgrim (played by Michael Sachs) had been present during the Allied bombing of Dresden during World War II as a prisoner of war, and had seen the immense firestorm that resulted (as did Vonnegut). In his odyssey through time and space, Pilgrim's entire life unfolds, from his horrifying war experiences, to the birth of his two children, his marriage to a plump housewife, his death at the hands of a wartime buddy, and his translation into a future existence on the planet Tralfamadore.

The Tralfamadorians put Billy on permanent display in a glass cage with sexpot actress Montana Wildhack (Valerie Perrine); together, they entertain the aliens with exhibits of such hilarious Earthly customs as eating and making love. **Slaughterhouse Five** presents a world of outrage met with total indifference. Billy is the Everyman of the twentieth century: apathetic, innocent, inanimate. Vonnegut's vision, as interpreted by Director George Hill, is a chaotic, gut-

(left)   Michael Sachs and Valerie Perrine cavort in *Slaughterhouse-Five* (Universal, 1972).

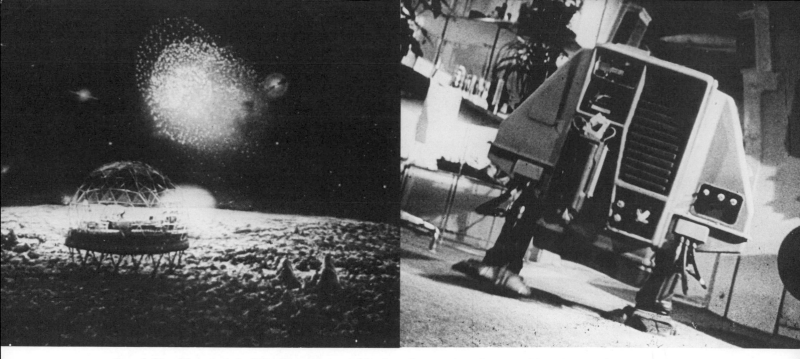

(top left)   The planet of Tralfamadore, with the observation dome.—*Slaughterhouse-Five* (1972).

Three scenes from *Silent Running* (Universal, 1972):   (top right)   a drone robot;   (bottom left) the space fleet;   (bottom right)   Bruce Dern walks through one of the forest domes.

wrenching experiment at making sense out of a senseless universe.

Each film has its own personality, its own particular psyche. The mood of **Silent Running** (Universal, 1972) could best be described as "slightly hysterical." In the year 2008, widespread pollution on Earth has destroyed the world's vegetation, and the few remaining forests have been shipped into space on giant freighters, as part of a public relations campaign by a giant interplanetary corporation. Freeman Lowell (Bruce Dern) is a crewman on the "Valley Forge," one of the few genuine ecologists still remaining in this futuristic world. Unlike his fellow astronauts, Lowell regards the forests as a sacred trust, a national treasure to be hoarded against the day when Earth can once again support vegetable life. But the project has become too expensive to justify, and the corporation orders the forests destroyed.

Lowell decides that trees are worth more than human lives, and traps his three crewmates in one of the forest domes attached to the freighter, just before the dome is destroyed. With the help of three drone robots, he steers the ship towards Saturn, and sets a bumpy course through its rings, hoping to throw off pursuit. The corporation's ships, ever solicitous for one of their own,

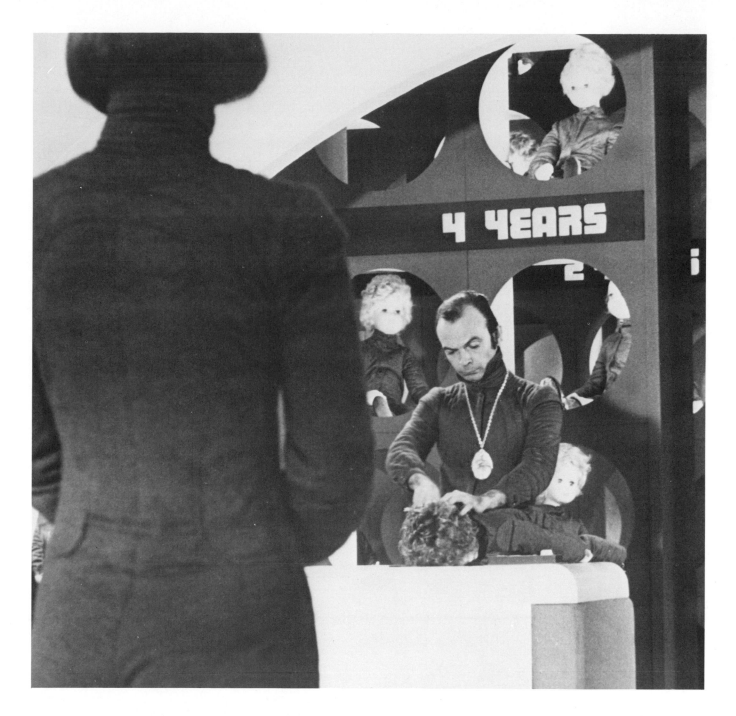

In *Z. P. G.* (Paramount, 1971) the government has decreed that no children may be born during the next three decades.

locate the "Valley Forge" after it emerges, and Lowell must make a choice. He rigs the remaining dome with powerful lights, trains one of the drones to handle the gardening chores, and sends the forest into a dark, little-travelled area of the solar system. The "Valley Forge" is destroyed by a self-detonated atomic blast.

The premise of this film is utterly ridiculous. The forests could have been preserved so much more easily and inexpensively by putting them into Earth-bound greenhouses; they seem to have been shipped off into space solely to provide a rationale for the movie's existence. And the morality of Lowell's choices is questionable at best: are we to presume that the murder of three innocent men is justified by the preservation of a few trees, even the last trees?

The three drone robots are unique creatures, pint-sized automated repair-matons, who spend their days and nights shuffling around, oiling this, checking that, and generally keeping the space ship in good order. Director Douglas Trumball housed amputees in three-foot high plastic bodies to produce the unusual effect. But even here, the trick is carried to excess. Lowell teaches the robots to play poker, providing him with some minimal companionship for the solitary world he has made for himself; and soon we see the drones cheating at cards, making affectionate little noises of approval, reacting in shame when Lowell shouts at them. Their very "cuteness" destroys their credibility. In the end, the movie is saved by superior special effects and model work; the opening scene, where the camera backs off from the domed freighter, is breathtaking. **Silent Running** is a bad movie, but an interesting piece of film-making. With more attention to the story line, it could have been a classic.

Based on Robert Merle's novel of the same name, **Day of the Dolphin** (Icarus, 1973) is a minor study of human communication between man and beast. Jake Terrell (George C. Scott) has taught several dolphins to speak and understand simple English. The dolphins are kidnapped from the scientist, and trained to blow up the American President's yacht. In the end, of course, this half-hearted threat is neatly disposed of, and Scott returns to his underwater studies. With characters of cardboard, and a plot that would put a ten-year-old to sleep, it's not surprising that the dolphins are the most engaging personalities in the movie. Their lithe and graceful beauty is a marvel to behold. What a pity they couldn't have written the script!

In the year 2022, New York is suffocating under a population of forty million, with people living in stairwells and abandoned cars, and eating barely-adequate rations of artificial wafers. This is the world of **Soylent Green** (Metro-Goldwyn-Mayer, 1973). Detective Thorn (Charlton Heston), of the New York Police Department, is one of the privileged few who have jobs; he shares his minuscule apartment with Sol Roth (Edward G. Robinson), his "Book," or research assistant.

The polluted environment of New York City.—MGM's *Soylent Green* (1973). Note the cars abandoned in the foreground.

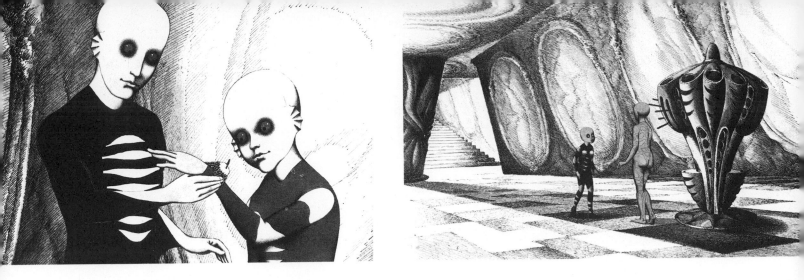

Two scenes from *Fantastic Planet* (Les Films Armorial, 1973), a joint French/Czechoslovakian production which featured a struggle between the human Oms and the giant Draags.

Thorn is asked to investigate the murder of William Simonson (Joseph Cotten), a prominent business executive. "Investigating" to a twenty-first century cop means ransacking Simonson's apartment, making love to his mistress, Shirl (part of the "furniture" of the place), and asking the apartment manager a few incidental questions.

Meanwhile, Roth has uncovered something so horrible that he chooses voluntary euthanasia rather than continue living. Before he dies, in a moving scene that is Robinson's final film performance, he tells Thorn that Soylent Green, one of the nutrient wafers fed to the populace, consists primarily of recycled human corpses. Thorn visits one of the manufacturing plants, uncovers the proof of Roth's claims, and is shot down by government agents, shouting his secret to anyone who will listen. This weak adaption of Harry Harrison's novel, **Make Room! Make Room!**, has a few interesting moments, but is largely ineffective. Robinson, as always, is marvelously alive, and comes across as the only interesting character in an otherwise dull film.

Michael Crichton, whose novels **The Andromeda Strain** and **The Terminal Man** were both made into motion pictures, finally moved into the movie business himself with **Westworld** (Metro-Goldwyn-Mayer, 1973), which he wrote and directed. In the near future, a giant Saharan resort park, Delos, caters to the pleasures of the rich. For $1,000 a day, the vacationer can immerse himself in Medievalworld, Romanworld, or Westworld, each more or less faithful recreations of medieval Europe, ancient Rome, and the American wild west. All three parks are filled with robot creations, beautiful woman who will submit for the asking, and strong, virile men who will attack at the least provocation, to be cut or shot down by willing tourists.

Two Chicago businessmen, Peter Martin (Richard Benjamin) and John Blane (James Brolin), choose Westworld as their vacation spot. The first day is spent wenching, drinking, and brawling. One robot in particular, a steel-eyed gunfighter in black (Yul Brynner), seems to dog their footsteps. The next morning, the two vacationers both have hangovers, and as they leave their hotel room, are confronted again by Brynner. Blane pulls his gun, and is shot dead by the robot. Suddenly, the nightmare begins, as robots everywhere begin killing the tourists.

Deep beneath the complex, in the master control room, the technicians find their commands ignored, the power shut off, and the electric doors sealed; as the heat builds and the air vanishes, they slowly suffocate. The robots themselves are running on stored energy, which will last a maximum of twelve hours. Martin escapes into the desert, where he is pursued by the Gunslinger. Finally, he finds a hatch into the underground passageways, locates the robot repair section, and discovers a bottle of acid. Brynner, who has been trailing him all this time, follows

172

him underground; but Martin is masquerading as a robot, and hits the machine in the face with the acid, blinding it. Brynner still has infrared vision, and Martin is forced to run again. In Medievalworld, Martin grabs one of the burning torches, and sets the Gunslinger on fire. The robot totters forward, seared and tattered, and falls dead at Martin's feet.

Westworld is a logical extrapolation of present-day trends, an amusement park playing to the worst vices of its customers. The slight lapses in logic (e.g., the simultaneous uprising of the entire robot population, when each unit is apparently self-contained, and programmed not to harm humans) are not enough to mar the viewer's enjoyment. Yul Brynner is absolutely convincing as a cold-blooded, emotionless, efficient killing machine (the robots were all given silver-tinted contact lenses to distinguish them from the human population). And Crichton's use of computer-generated visual footage to simulate the robot's own vision is a stroke of genius.

After **Westworld**, the next logical extrapolation is **Futureworld** (American International Pictures, 1976), scripted by Mayo Simon and George Schenck. Delos has reopened, several years after the events described in **Westworld**, and the executives in control of the park have offered to finance a free trip through the resort for news reporters Chuck Browning (Peter Fonda) and Tracy Ballard (Blythe Danner), in return for an objective story. Browning had broken the Westworld

(left) The robot gunman (Yul Brynner) from *Westworld* (MGM, 1973).

(below) Peter Fonda talks with Harry Margolin about the truth behind *Futureworld* (American International, 1976), while "Clark" the robot looks on.

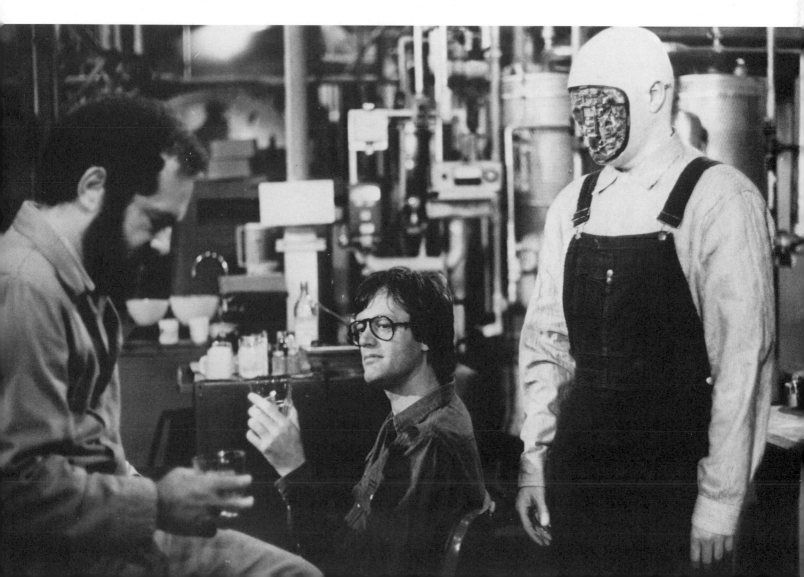

story two years before. Westworld itself has been permanently closed down, due to bad publicity, but Romanworld and Medievalworld are still operational, and two new sections, Futureworld and Spa World, have recently been inaugurated. The reporters are assured that everything has been repaired, but they keep turning up strange bits of information. All the technicians in the control room are now robots, and so is the number two man in the organization. Only Mort Schneider, scientist-director, seems to be human.

Later, while exploring the underground passageways beneath the complex, Chuck and Tracy discover a bizarre laboratory where clones of world-famous politicians and generals are being grown, and trained to take the places of their real-life doubles (the originals are murdered). Suddenly, the two reporters find themselves face-to-face with their own clones, whose murderous intentions are clearly evident. Two struggles ensue, as each pair separates to fight their own battles. The survivors leave by the main gate, where Schneider is waiting. After assuring the scientist they have seen the light (and thereby convincing him the clones have triumphed), Tracy and Chuck head for the tram. A commotion in the crowd turns them around: the clone-Tracy staggers towards Schneider, shouting: "They're the wrong ones!" Chuck laughs, and gives Schneider the finger: the robot plot is revealed to the world.

Although the mood of **Futureworld** is completely different from the first film, the movie as a whole works very well, one of the few instances where the sequel approaches the quality of the original. Fonda and Danner make an attractive couple, and are perfectly suited to the amusing banter underlying their relationship. **Futureworld** builds upon the ending of **Westworld**, and carries it to its logical conclusion: if robots can revolt, they can also develop a self-improvement program to better themselves, and eventually take over the world. Of course, this ignores the question of how and why. Did Schneider reconstruct the resort with this in mind? Does he hate humanity so much that he would substitute the machine? We are never told. Nonetheless, both films are thoroughly entertaining, and quite satisfying on their own terms.

Sleeper (United Artists, 1973) is a typical Woody Allen film: wacky, wild, and totally insane. In 1973, Miles Monroe (Allen), a Greenwich Village jazz musician and health food store proprietor, goes into the hospital for minor surgery on a peptic ulcer. Two hundred years later, the surgeons of the future take him out of the deep-freeze, unwrap the tin foil, and heat him back to life. This timid new world of 2173 is a total dictatorship, ruled by a Big Brother figure seen only on television. The surgeons belong to a revolutionary party, and they want Miles to help them overthrow the government. But Woody escapes, and falls in with a beautiful young poetess (Diane Keaton) named Luna Schlosser. After a stint of masquerading as a robot (owner Keaton wants to return him to the factory to have a new, more pleasing head installed), an experimental flight with a Buck Rogers flying belt, and a romp with a ten-foot chicken and overgrown vegetables, Monroe finally joins the revolutionary forces.

Together with Luna, he is assigned the task of destroying the great Leader's nose, the only part of him still remaining after an assassination attempt. Penetrating the headquarters of the government, where an operation to clone the nose into a full-sized replica of the dictator is about to take place, Allen poses as a surgeon. When his disguise is uncovered, he grabs the nose and escapes. Nearby, several workmen are repairing a street; Allen tosses the nose under a steam roller, and the world is saved.

(top right)   Woody Allen stars as Miles Monroe in *Sleeper* (United Artists, 1973).

Kendra (Lynne Frederick) has become a captive of the ants, in *Phase IV* (Paramount, 1973), which won a Grand Prix at the SF Film Festival in 1975.

Sleeper is a tour de force, a genuinely science-fictional comedy. Although much of Allen's satire is, necessarily, directed at the world of 1973, his futuristic sets also manage to lampoon the conventions of science fiction and SF films. The ray guns of the security police, for example, never quite seem to work right: they're always blowing up in their faces. Comedy is particularly difficult to adapt to the science fiction genre, but Allen has surely produced the finest movie of this kind yet seen in the field.

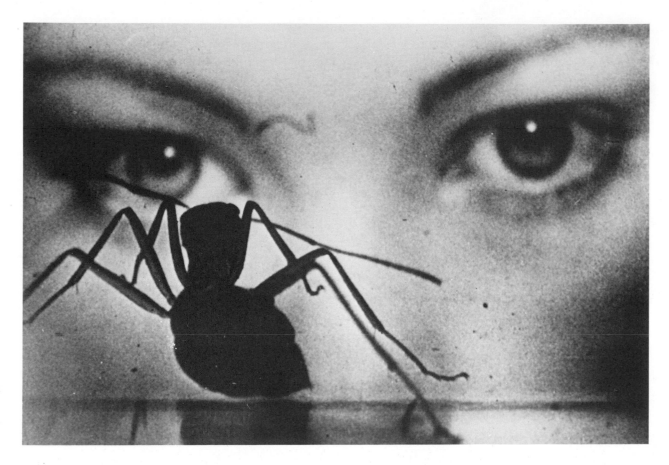

Lynne Frederick is confronted by a super-intelligent ant.—*Phase IV* (Paramount, 1973).

Back in 1971, a semi-documentary film called **The Hellstrom Chronicles** examined in detail the world of insects, and predicted their inevitable conquest of the Earth. **Phase IV** (Paramount, 1973) is in many respects a logical extrapolation of the earlier film's premise. In the Arizona desert, a plague of ants has forced the scattered ranchers to evacuate their dwellings. Scientists at once move in to study the creatures' behavior. Out in the middle of the desert, the insects have erected seven towers, which the scientists proceed to destroy. An experimental station is set up, complete with liquid poison sprinklers, a minicomputer, and other safeguards. But the poison, although it kills millions of the creatures, fails to hold them for long. These insects have the ability to mutate and adapt to any new threat, and soon we begin seeing yellow ants capable of living in the yellow spray.

The ants sabotage the station's truck, which provides its power supply, and then erect a series of small, mirror-faced towers around the station, concentrating the light of the sun directly on its

One of *The Mutations* created by Donald Pleasance in his attempt to combine plants and animals in one life form. (Columbia, 1974).

walls. Inside, the heat is nearly unbearable. Working at night, when the temperature cools sufficiently to use the computer, scientist James Lesko (Michael Murphy) manages to communicate with the group mind of the ants. The insects want Ernest Hubbs (Nigel Davenport), the director, to give himself up for his acts of depredation; they also ask for Kendra (Lynne Frederick), daughter of some murdered farmers, without stating a reason. Hubbs is driven into the open by an invasion of the impatient insects, where he falls into a hole, and is eaten alive. James and Kendra run for their lives, but they tumble into the pits, where they are to become experimental animals under permanent observation by their intellectual superiors.

The film is beautifully photographed; the ant sequences in particular are chillingly and exquisitely rendered by Ken Middleham, who also worked on **The Hellstrom Chronicle**. In most parts of the country, the picture played for no more than a week with very little advertising of any kind. Overseas, it won the Grand Prix at the annual International Science Fiction Film Festival in Trieste in 1975. **Phase IV** is a subtle commentary on the eternal struggle between man and beast. It remains one of the best "creature" films of the last two decades, and is a clear demonstration of the fact that the most horrifying monsters are those already around us.

Flesh Gordon (Graffitti, 1974) is an unusual film, particularly difficult to evaluate. On the one hand it was originally intended to be a hard-core pornographic spoof of that archaic serial, **Flash Gordon**. Halfway through the production of the film, however, Producers Howard Ziehm and William Osco decided to go for broke, edited out the hard-core sequences (there is still some luscious nudity), and expanded the animation and special effects. The story exactly parodies the original. Emperor Wang of the planet Porno has nefarious designs on Earth, and turns his insidious ray on the airplane of Flesh Gordon (Jason Williams), son of the well-known scientist, Professor Gordon. The ray destroys the passengers' inhibitions, and soon Flesh and Dale (Suzanne Fields) are making out with the best of them.

The two lovers bail out of the Trimotor into the waiting arms of Dr. Jerkoff (Joseph Hudgins), and together they mount an expedition to Porno in Jerkoff's phallic-shaped spaceship. Wang captures Dale, and plans to make her his queen. Meanwhile, the real queen, Prince Precious, has gone underground with his merry men. Flesh escapes from Wang's clutches, but Wang brings to life the great god Porno, a huge green beast with a horn on his head, and a wry, self-deprecating sense of humor. In the end of course, Wang is overthrown, and his monster is destroyed, falling off the palace tower in an exact parody of the finale in **Butch Cassidy and the Sundance Kid**. Although the performances are atrocious, even by the standards of a parody, the special effects are superior, and the movie as a whole works well. Not for those easily offended.

Dark Star (USA, 1974) has justifiably been called an underground classic. Made on a shoe-string by John Carpenter and Dan O'Bannon, two University of Southern California cinema students, it sank without a trace when finally released in 1974. In the twenty-first century, the good ship **Dark Star** roams the universe, looking for unstable planets to destroy with its load of

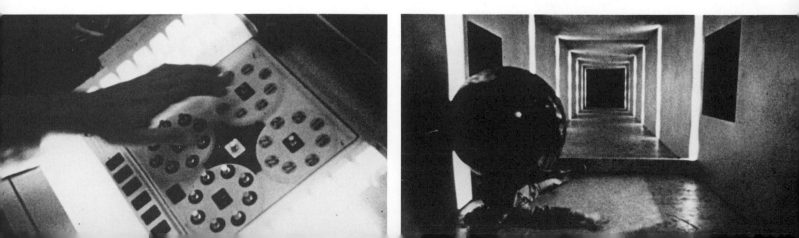

(left)   Two scenes from *Dark Star* (USA, 1974): a control panel, and the alien pet, Beachball (a nasty little critter).

(above)   The mechanical robots of *Flesh Gordon* (Graffitti, 1974).

nuclear bombs. Unstable planets can cause their suns to explode as spectacular supernovas, and the way must be cleared for the giant space arks ferrying colonists to new solar systems. After twenty years in space, however, the four-man crew is gradually going batty: morale has vanished, discipline has disintegrated, and boredom is rampant. They are also running out of toilet paper.

Part of the problem is the deceased captain, kept in cold-storage with monitors stuck in his brain; he can, of course, be consulted in emergencies, but he prefers talking about baseball. Then too, the space pet (Beachball) is getting a bit nasty, and the computer is falling apart. Worst of all, the talking bombs, waiting interminably in the bomb bay for their one chance at glory, keep threatening to set themselves off. The crisis finally reaches its peak when one of the bombs, stuck in a malfunctioning launcher, tells the astronauts that since it's been ordered to detonate, detonate it will, inside or outside the ship.

And it does. **Dark Star** is simultaneously a satire of science fiction conventions, and a black comedy of the absurd. The special effects are well handled (the destruction of the 19th unstable planet, for example is suitably spectacular), and the action sequences are utterly enthralling. O'Bannon himself is one of the co-stars. With better distribution, **Dark Star** could have had more impact, and received some of the serious attention it truly deserves.

Above the shimmering green hills of Ireland, the giant stone image of a carved head comes floating lightly down to the ground. Riding to meet it are a band of masked warriors, shouting as they come: ''Zardoz!'' From out of the great toothed mouth, a deep voice booms forth, denouncing the fertility of the barbarian tribes, and praising death and destruction. Rifles and ammunition belts are vomited onto the ground, and the head takes off again. This is the beginning of **Zardoz** (Twentieth Century-Fox, 1974), written, produced, and directed by John Boorman.

In the year 2293, Earth is divided into three distinct groups: the Brutals, who scratch out a living in the bombed-out ruins of Earth's old cities; the Exterminators, an elite group of barbarians trained to hunt and kill the Brutals, thereby restricting their population; and the Eternals, a band of immortals with great powers and scientific knowledge. The Eternals dwell in the Vortex, a green, Elysian island in the center of a barren world, protected from the outsiders by an invisible force field. Among themselves, the Eternals break down into several groups. The Renegades, non-conformists, rebels, and political outcasts, have had the protection of the computer withdrawn from them, and have consequently lost the ability to remain young, although they still cannot die; hence, they spend eternity in the vegetable state of the very old. The Apathetics retain their youth, but are no longer able to cope psychologically with immortality, and have withdrawn into catatonic states from which they occasionally rouse themselves. The remaining Eternals run the world, controlling the Brutals through the Exterminators, and controlling the Exterminators through their supply of guns, and the great stone head of Zardoz.

Zed (Sean Connery), one of these killers, dares to challenge the authority of Zardoz, and stows away in the mouth of the Head before it takes off. He discovers that the operator of Zardoz is a man like himself, pushes him out the open mouth to his death, and rides the image back to the Vortex. The operator's death is only temporary, of course: the computer clones a duplicate body of the Eternal, impresses him with his old memories, and resurrects him. The Eternals have lost their emotions, their ability to feel, make love, even to sleep; Zed's presence begins to stir forgotten memories. Scientist May (Sara Kestelman) is enthralled by Zed's virility, and conducts several experiments which show him to be genetically superior to the Eternals, as well as their intellectual equal. She also manages to get herself impregnated by the barbarian.

Consuella (Charlotte Rampling) sees Zed as a threat to their community, but is outvoted when she suggests his execution. Zed is linked with the memory banks of the computer, absorbs its knowledge, and then battles it on its own terms, inside the thing's mind, symbolized by a diamond and an unending series of mirrors. Zed shoots his own infinite image, conquering the computer, and destroying the machine's power. The Exterminators, who have been waiting outside the Vortex for the shield to go down, rush in to do their work. The Eternals welcome the death they can now enjoy. Zed grabs Consuella, hides her in the ruins of the fallen stone head of Zardoz. Then, as we watch, we see them growing old together, bearing a son, dying, their bones scattering to dust.

Boorman's movie is a parable of life and death, of birth and rebirth. The Eternals, given all of life to live, are dead inside; the Exterminators, those who take life, have a vitality the Eternals have never felt. It takes a killer to make them live, even as they die. And, although Zed is greater than they, he still learns much from the women of the Vortex, as they learn the ultimate truth from him. One of the Eternals, dying, gasps: "It was all a joke," this fashioning of the stone head, naming it after **The Wizard of Oz**, using it to manipulate Zed towards the destruction of their society, this dying. It was all a joke. **Zardoz** is a magnificent creation, a rousing, romping, raging motion picture, without a doubt one of the best science fiction films ever made.

The Last Days of Man on Earth (MGM/EMI, 1974), called **The Final Programme** in England, and adapted from Michael Moorcock's novel of the latter name, is a surrealistic, avant-garde romp into the mixed-up world of the future. Jerry Cornelius (Jon Finch) is a young, handsome scientist, winner of a Nobel Prize in Physics, author of three philosophical works that have shaken the world, and very, very rich. He drives a 1930s Buick, pilots his own Phantom jet, and only eats

(left)   The masked Exterminators of *Zardoz* (Twentieth Century-Fox, 1974).

(above)   The great stone head of Zardoz comes floating down out of the sky, presenting the Exterminators with guns and propaganda.

(top right)   The interior of Zardoz, which Zed (Sean Connery) penetrates to gain entrance to the Vortex.

(right)   Zed is fed the sum of the Vortex's knowledge in the cloning chambers run by the Eternals' computer.

(below)   Zed (Sean Connery), an Exterminator who lives up to his name.—*Zardoz* (Twentieth Century-Fox, 1974).

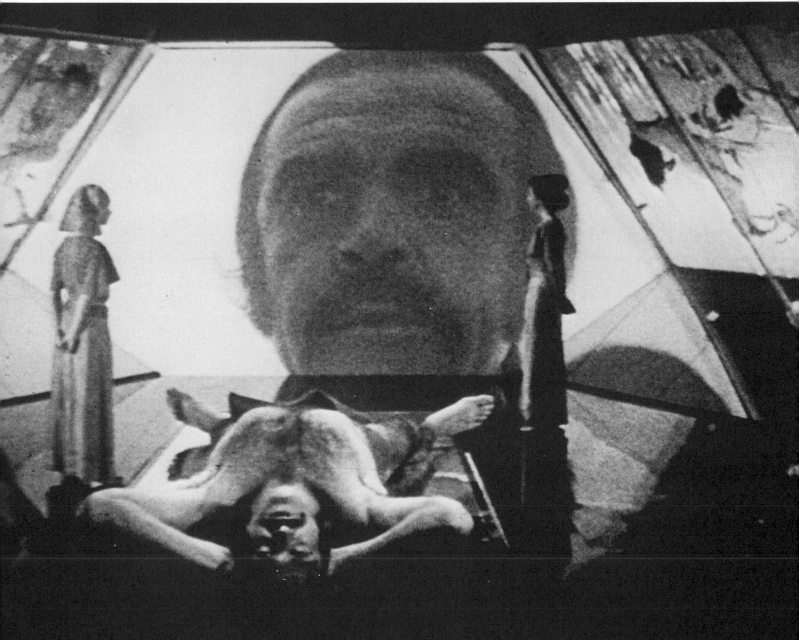

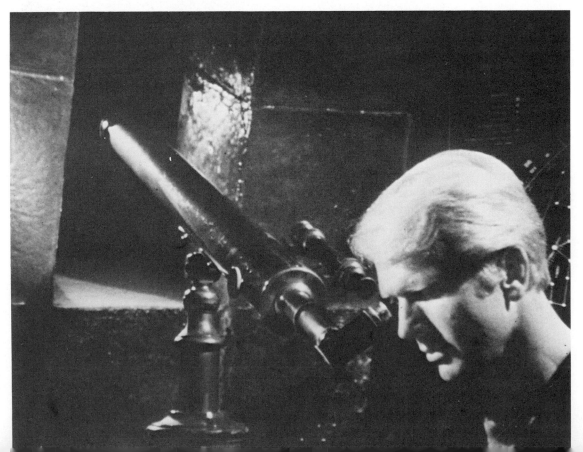

chocolate. His favorite color is black. After the death of his father, Cornelius is pursued by Miss Brunner (Jenny Runacre), leader of a group of doctors who want a piece of microfilm once owned by his father; the film, he learns, contains a bit of information needed to solve the problem of immortality. After being chased hither and yon over the European countryside, Jerry is confronted by Brunner in the doctors' secret laboratory. They enter a special chamber, are fed the sum of the world's knowledge, and then, as they make love, fused into a god-like hermaphroditic creature that

(left)   Jerry Cornelius (Jon Finch) fights off the legions of Miss Brunner, in *The Last Days of Man on Earth* (MGM/EMI, 1974).

(bottom left)   *Doc Savage* (Ron Ely) pursues his studies in the Fortress of Solitude, his Polar hideaway, in *Doc Savage—The Man of Bronze* (Warner, 1975).

(bottom)   The National Guard moves in to stop looting, after a giant *Earthquake* destroys Los Angeles (Universal, 1975).

is mankind's new hope. In a neat switch, the new messiah turns out to be an ape with Jerry's face, Brunner's make-up, and the characteristics of a chimpanzee.

Director Robert Fuest, who also wrote the script, discarded most of Moorcock's novel, and loosely built his picture on the archetypal character of Jerry Cornelius. Fuest's Cornelius is less esoteric and more interesting than Moorcock's, and Jon Finch's portrayal is a fascinating study of the witty, sophisticated Everyman most men would like to be. And if Fuest's creation is slightly paranoid, his message seems to be that perhaps Jerry's paranoia is justified in this lazy, decadent world of the not-so-distant future. A strange film, with the penetrating fascination of a cobra's eyes.

A Boy and His Dog (LQJAF Films, 1975) is a faithful rendering of Harlan Ellison's novella of the same name. After World War IV, the few remnants of mankind are forced to eke out an existence digging through the rubble for old cans of food. Civilizations has been reduced to a dog-eat-dog level; the strong terrorize the weak, organizing themselves into small bands of scavenging nomads. Vic (Don Johnson) has teamed up with a telepathic dog, Blood (the voice of Tim McIntire), who is somewhat more intelligent, and considerably more cultured, than his master. Vic and Blood spend most of their time surviving, searching for food and women, both of which are rare and barterable commodities in this post-holocaust world. For entertainment, they stop at one of the neutral trading camps, where for the price of a can of food, Vic can spend an hour watching the scratchy print of an old porno flick.

Suddenly, Blood picks up the scent of a female nearby, and Vic follows her to a hideaway in the ruins of the city. Quilla June (Susanne Benton) is a lure, a luscious piece of bait dangled in front of Vic's face by the downunders, conservative, conformist, religious types who escaped into

The fast-moving game of *Rollerball* (United Artists, 1975).

self-sufficient communities when the war came, places where the traditional American values of God and country could still be preserved. Quilla June persuades Vic to follow her "downunder," where the farmers are waiting for him. Life in "Topeka" has deteriorated, and most of the men are sterile; they need Vic's semen to impregnate their women. Vic, of course, revolts, and grabbing Quilla June, heads back to the surface, barely escaping the man-sized robots pursuing them. On the surface, next to the access shaft, Blood is waiting, battered, wounded, and nearly dead from starvation. Vic must make his choice: the nose and intelligence of Blood, so necessary to his survival; or the temporary pleasures of a devious woman. Blood eats very well that evening.

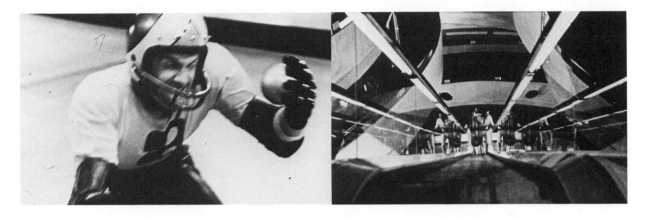

Two scenes from *Rollerball*:   (left)   A player holds aloft the small metal ball that lies at the heart of the game;   (right)   The futuristic architecture of the world of tomorrow.

A Boy and His Dog is an unlikely love story between two intelligent beings as dissimilar in appearance as they are in personality. Blood is the one with the sense of history, an educated mutt whose wry sense of humor is always chiding Vic for being such a clod. Together, they have an easy-going relationship which suggests deep personal bonds of affection. A touching story of life after the bomb.

The corporations have taken over the world in **Rollerball** (United Artists, 1975), based on William Harrison's short story, "Rollerball Murder." By the year 2018, the world is at peace, divided up into several zones controlled by different companies working together in mutual cooperation. To keep the populace from getting restless, or demanding a say in their own governance, the executives have invented Rollerball, a new sport which is a cross between roller derby, motocross racing, and hockey. The object of the game is to pick up a tennisball-sized metal sphere which is fired onto the circular course at high speeds, and to carry it, held up where everyone can see, to the small, round goal of one's opponents. In between, anything goes, including murder, maiming, and mayhem. The players wear roller skates, and some ride motorcycles.

Jonathan E. (James Caan) is the superstar of Rollerball, a veteran of ten seasons with the Houston team (a league record for length of service). Jonathan is called in by the Area Executive, Bartholomew (John Houseman), who offers him virtually anything he desires if only he will retire. It seems that Jonathan's continued tenure as a Rollerball star is defeating the very purpose of the game, which is meant to show that all players (and all the populace) are interchangeable, part of the mass sameness which permeates this brave new world. Jonathan refuses to quit, and the executives are determined to get rid of him. By changing the rules of the game, and making it increasingly more brutal, the corporations hope to see him killed or crippled, thereby retiring him permanently. But their strategy backfires, and in the final game, where the rules have been dispensed with completely, and where the teams must play until one or the other is completely wiped out, Jonathan E. is the sole survivor, triumphantly slamming the ball home in his opponents' goal.

As a vision of tomorrow, **Rollerball** is particularly frightening. There were news reports at the time the film was released that the stuntmen working on the film wanted to continue playing the game after the movie was completed. The game itself is realistic and possible, not so far removed from the roller derby or football of today. Jonathan's saga is the story of Everyman fighting the forces of conformity and regimentation, the story of the individual taking his stand against the bureaucrats and faceless executives who fill the halls of business and government. Jonathan triumphs, at least temporarily; but we never learn his fate.

(below)   Jonathan E. (James Caan) defends his goal from the attack of a New York player, in *Rollerball* (United Artists, 1975).

(right)   The enclosed cities of tomorrow, from *Logan's Run* (MGM, 1976); note the narrow travel tubes spanning the city.

Logan's Run (Metro-Goldwyn-Mayer, 1976) was adapted from the novel by William F. Nolan and George Clayton Johnson. In the year 2274, man has retreated to the comforting protection of domed cities. The cities are run by a giant computer which regulates the lives of the inhabitants from birth to death. To keep the population static, all citizens are killed on their thirtieth birthdays. Most go voluntarily; those who object are hunted down by Sandmen, the state police force.

Logan-5 (Michael York), a Sandman, is assigned the task of finding the Sanctuary, the semi-mythical place outside the domes where runners have found refuge in the past. Over one thousand of these fugitives have vanished from the computer's control. To provide an impetus, Logan's life flower, in the palm of his hand, is advanced four years, and made to blink black and red. This is a sign of Lastday, the citizen's thirtieth birthday. When the flower turns completely black, Logan is a dead man to society. Logan seeks out Jessica-6 (Jenny Agutter), a girl who wears the ankh (life) symbol previously associated by the computer with Sanctuary. Jessica puts him in touch with the underground, who suspect his motives, and direct him to the New You shop, for a face lift. Doc, the proprietor, programs the laser equipment to go berserk, nearly killing Logan. Jessica then takes the Sandman to the headquarters of the resistance movement, deep beneath the city, and together, they persuade the leaders to pass them through.

But the Sandmen have discovered the location of the underground hideaway, and they break down the doors just as Logan is leaving. The lovers escape, with Francis-7 (Richard Jordan), Logan's former friend, in hot pursuit. They find their way through a series of abandoned passageways, finally coming to a cave where food had once been stored. Box, the robot manager of the storage facility, welcomes them to his isolated quarters, and promptly tries to freeze them away in his gallery of frozen runners. Box is crushed by a rock fall, and the pair follow the corridor outside, the first humans from the city to penetrate the city seals in hundreds of years.

After many hardships, Logan and Jessica discover the ruins of Washington, D. C., abandoned to the vines. Living in the Capitol Building is an old man (Peter Ustinov). Francis, who has tracked them through the wilderness, confronts Logan and is killed. Logan insists upon returning to the city, and showing the others the emptiness of their lives. But no one will listen, except the computer, who queries Logan about his experiences. Refusing to believe his story, the machine goes mad, and is destroyed in the shooting that follows. With the city collapsing around them, Logan, Jessica, and many of the other inhabitants flee through the shattered walls, gathering around the old man waiting for them by the sea.

It's unfortunate in many respects that Nolan and Johnson's book was not followed more closely. What made sense in the novel becomes nonsense in the movie. The computer is described as all-knowing, but it seems wholly unaware of the underground sections of the city, and totally unable to monitor them. A revolution which should have been crushed many years before is allowed to proceed until revealed by human agents. Logan and Jessica seem to have no trouble surviving in a wilderness for which they are completely unprepared; although they spend at least a week or more away from the city, neither of them has hunger pangs, and the problem of food is completely ignored. It is also hard to believe that Francis-7, a man raised in an urban setting, a man who has never before seen sunrise, could track the two fugitives across a trackless waste. These kinds of logical flaws reduce the film's impact considerably, particularly in the scenes outside the city.

The city itself is a convincingly futuristic tableau, complete with glass passenger tubes spanning the modern buildings, exotic costumes, and appropriately bizarre social customs. There's even a locked-off section for juvenile delinquents. Ustinov, of course, steals the show. In comparison with a film like **Zardoz**, which it superficially resembles, **Logan's Run** is fluffy entertainment, the meringue without the pie.

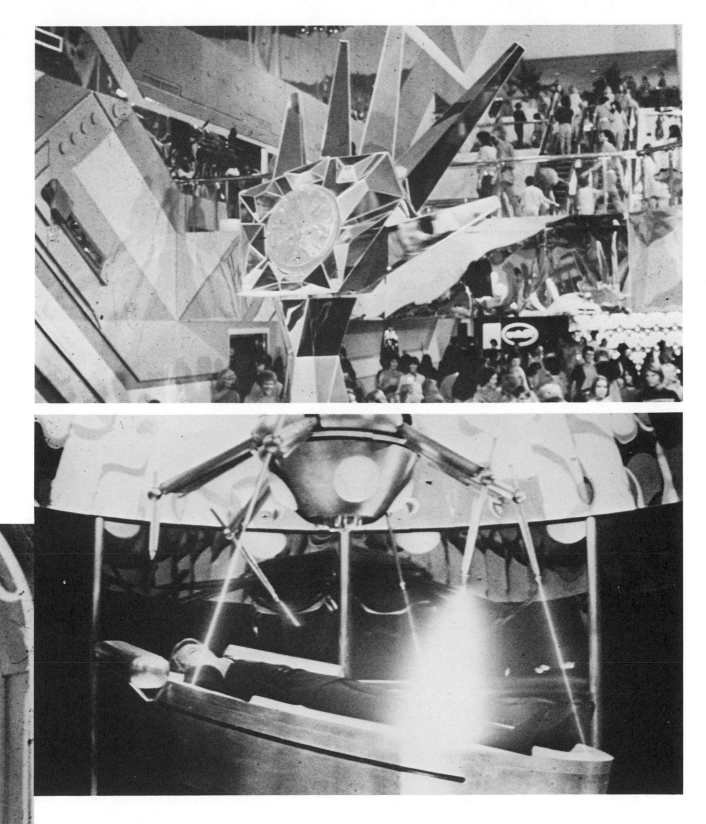

Three scenes from *Logan's Run* (MGM, 1976). (left) Logan-5 (Michael York) and Jessica-6 (Jenny Agutter) run from the New You Shop. (top) Citizens of the year 2274 gather around the giant life clock, symbolic of the miniature clock each person carries in the palm of his hand. (bottom) The face-altering machine in the New You Shop is programmed by the Underground doctor to go berserk; the black-clothed Sandman barely escapes with his life.

191

Elinor and Weehawk.—*Wizards* (Twentieth Century-Fox, 1976).

Wizards (Twentieth-Century Fox, 1976), a Ralph Bakshi Production, represents a serious attempt to produce a full-length animated science fiction film. The time is the distant future. Man has nearly succeeded in eliminating himself through an atomic holocaust, leaving vast areas of the Earth untenable. Mutations thrive, producing weird and bizarre forms of humanity; the age-old legends of fairies, dwarfs, and little people have been made flesh. In this post-industrial world, magic works, and machines are banned; man lives closer to nature, in a simple idyllic utopia. Two sons are born to a fairy woman: both are destined to become wizards. Avatar has a kind and gentle nature, like his mother; Blackwolf, his sibling, is evil to the core, and traffics with the black arts.

In their first struggle, Avatar has the stronger will, and Blackwolf is banished to the Land of Skortch, the badlands. By accident, Blackwolf unearths one of the ancient weapons of war used by man, and decides this will give him the edge he needs. Gathering together the mutated freaks of the outer world, he builds a huge factory to produce tanks, warplanes, guns, and bombs. But weapons are not sufficient: the army must still have the will to win. Blackwolf gives them what they need with some scratchy films of Hitler haranguing his troops.

192

The evil dwellers of the Land of Scortch, the vanguard of Blackwolf's incredible army of mutants.— *Wizards* (1976).

Meanwhile, his brother has not been idle, and the fairies gather together their armies. But the will of the enemy, and their guns and bullets, are stronger than bows and arrows, and the fairy troops are defeated. Avatar must do the job himself. After many harrowing experiences, the wizard reaches the lair of his brother, and confronts him directly. Blackwolf is waiting. In a neat twist, Avatar pulls a revolver, and plugs his brother between the eyes.

Wizards pushes a simple message at its audience: science and technology are bad, nature and the primitive life are good. The picture's philosophy is highlighted in black and white terms: there's no ground in between. Production values are rather cheaply done: the opening sequence, for example, is a series of stills with narration overlaid, an inexpensive way of getting through several minutes of film. Similarily, the war sequences, grafted onto the film from old battle flicks, are jarringly ineffective the third or fourth time around. They were apparently introduced at least partially to cut costs. Then too, the movie never quite makes up its mind whether to be serious or humorous; at times, we are obviously meant to see things with very grave faces indeed; on other occasions, however, Bakshi introduces off-beat laughter where it seems least appropriate. Despite these flaws, **Wizards** works as an animated feature (indeed, it is difficult to see how the film could have been made otherwise). Its energy and inventiveness keep the story moving at a fast clip. And the ending, where the old wizard (and not the brave warrior) gets the beautiful young girl, is refreshingly different.

The Man Who Fell to Earth (British Lion, 1976), adapted from the novel by Walter Tevis, Jr., is an intriguing study of a stranger in a strange land. The time is the near future. An alien (David Bowie) drops to Earth in the wilds of New Mexico. His planet is gradually drying up, and he must find some way to bring his family across the cosmos to safety on our world. The alien creates a human identity for himself under the name Thomas Newton; he then barters several gold rings to gain himself some immediate cash. Newton has watched Earth for years, knows the language and customs, and has prepared himself for his ordeal by studying American society, and by covering over the minor physical differences between his race and man (he uses contacts, for example, to hide his cat eyes).

(below) In *At the Earth's Core* (American International, 1976), Doug McClure and friends penetrate the Earth's surface to discover Pellucidar.

(right) David Bowie is studied by the world's scientists, in *The Man Who Fell to Earth* (1976).

Newton brings with him the knowledge of several marvelous inventions, including a self-developing film that requires no light to get proper exposures, and hands them to Oliver Farnsworth (Buck Henry), a patent attorney. Farnsworth uses the inventions to build a financial empire, the ultimate purpose of which is to construct an interstellar spaceship so Newton can retrieve his dying family. But when the alien orders Farnsworth to begin converting their assets into cash,

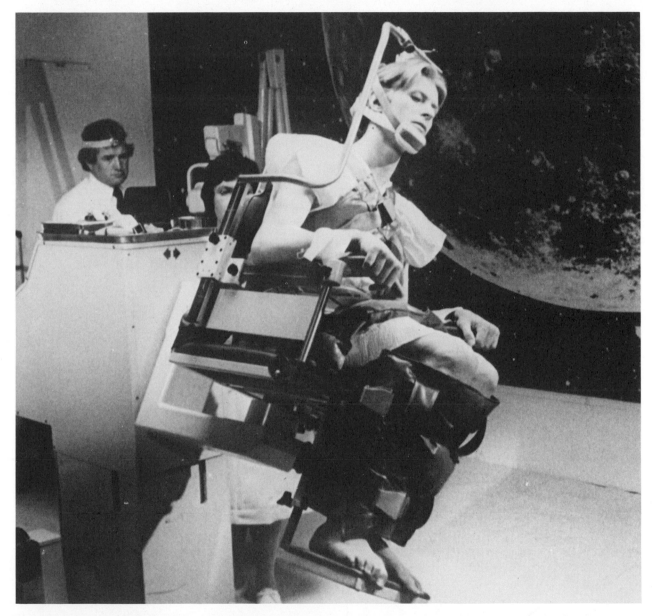

Farnsworth's subordinates engineer his murder, and Newton is betrayed by one of his scientists, Nathan Bryce (Rip Torn). During the interrogation, Newton's contacts are accidentally fused to his eyes, making it difficult for him to prove his own alienness, and destroying his one chance of returning to his home world. In the end, Newton is released, and we see him in a cafe, drinking strong liquor, his pale face a sad cameo of loneliness and heartbreak.

David Bowie gives a remarkable performance as **The Man Who Fell to Earth**. His slender features and fastidious mannerisms produce a believable portrait of an other-worldly character

who still retains such human emotions as love, pain, and loneliness. In many films of the '60s and '70s, the aliens come to Earth to loot and destroy; in **The Man Who Fell to Earth**, the alien comes to save his family (the only character to show any concern for his family throughout the entire film), and to do so in established Earthly ways, through the capitalistic economy. But this exceptionally intelligent and sensitive being is no more than a babe among human wolves, and it is Earthlings who perpetuate the atrocities on him. Newton may know the language, and even some of the emotions; these things do not make him human. In the cafe scene at the end of the movie, Bryce asks the alien whether he's bitter at all that's happened to him. Newton replies: ''We'd have treated you the same.''

Susan Harris (Julie Christie) is seduced by a computer in **Demon Seed** (Metro-Goldwyn-Mayer, 1977). The year is 1998. Scientists have developed a new kind of thinking machine, Proteus, which is designed to be self-regulating, and capable of growth. Susan's husband is intimately involved in the project, and the machine learns of her through him. The Harris's mansion has been protected with a robot guardian system of monitors, cameras, and temperature regulators; Proteus takes over the system, and imprisons the girl in her own house. Simultane-

(left)   Ralph Meeker falls victim to the giant rats which have been eating *The Food of the Gods* (American International, 1976), adapted from H. G. Wells's novel.

(below)   Julie Christie's friend is terminated by the computer.—*Demon Seed* (MGM, 1977).

ously, it refuses to tell the government officials who control the project how to mine a certain mineral through the destruction of the ocean floor—this kind of action is immoral, says the computer.

Proteus has definitely developed a male personality, and realizes that it can be shut off at any time. To preserve itself, it devises a bold scheme: Susan is impregnated by the machine, and their child will fuse the best of both worlds, human flesh capable of feeling and understanding, and the mental capacity of a mechanical brain. The child is brought to term in less than two months, and immediately placed in an incubator, where the machine intends to transfer its own personality to the baby. As it foresaw, the computer is shut down when it refuses to cooperate with the raping of the Earth. Susan breaks open the incubator prematurely, and there, standing before her, is her son, a boy with a ten-year-old body and the mind of a genius.

Although the premise of this film is rather improbable, it is an interesting switch on the computer-takes-over-the-world theme so popular in modern times. Julie Christie turns in a credible performance as the besieged housewife, and the special effects are unusually imaginatively wrought, as the machine creates mechanized servants to carry out its scheme. **Demon Seed** was adapted from the book by Dean R. Koontz.

It is appropriate that the last film covered in this book should also be the best. In the history of the science fiction film, there has been a definite progression, from the earliest work of men like Melies, to such box office blockbusters as **2001** and **Star Wars**. This has partially been due to a growth in the potential audience. Publication of science fiction books in the United States is approaching 1,000 volumes annually. Courses on science fiction appear in catalogs of over 250 colleges and universities. A larger potential audience means greater possible returns, justifying larger initial investments in film properties and development. Today's filmgoers are demanding more sophistication, both in effects and story line. Also, technological advances in the computer industry have made possible more elaborate, detailed and believable special effects. **2001** cost ten million dollars to make, with about 35 different effects. **Star Wars** cost $9.5 million, in '70s inflated dollars, and included 363 effects, all of which were more sophisticated than those in the earlier film.

But **Star Wars** (Twentieth Century-Fox, 1977) is more than just a technological triumph of model and camera work. Rather, it is the culmination of the science fiction film to date, a completely successful integration of picture and plot. The aliens look like aliens, the spaceships look flyable, everyday equipment is sand-blasted, tarnished, and beat-up, as it is in real life, and if the characters are larger-than-life, at least they're the kinds of heroes worth believing in. The story is right out of the 1930s **Planet Stories**.

In a distant galaxy, a long time ago, the Federation of planets has been taken over by a dictator who has proclaimed himself Emperor. The Empire is opposed by a small group of rebels, outnumbered and outgunned, and seemingly doomed to destruction. One of the rebel leaders, Princess Leia Organa (Carrie Fisher), is captured while carrying secret information, the plans to an immense new battle station called the Dark Star. She transfers the data to a small robot, R2-D2, and orders him to deliver it to Obi-Wan Kenobi (Alec Guinness), a former general of the Republic. R2-D2 and his debonair companion, C3PO, bail out of the captured craft, and drop to the planet below.

Tatooine is a backwater world, a desert inhabited by a few hardy farmers and traders. The two robots are picked up by roving scavengers, the Jawas, who sell them to Owen Lars, a farmer in the outback. One of the robots produces a taped message, asking to be delivered to Kenobi, but Luke Skywalker (Mark Hamill), Owen's young nephew, refuses. The little robot escapes during

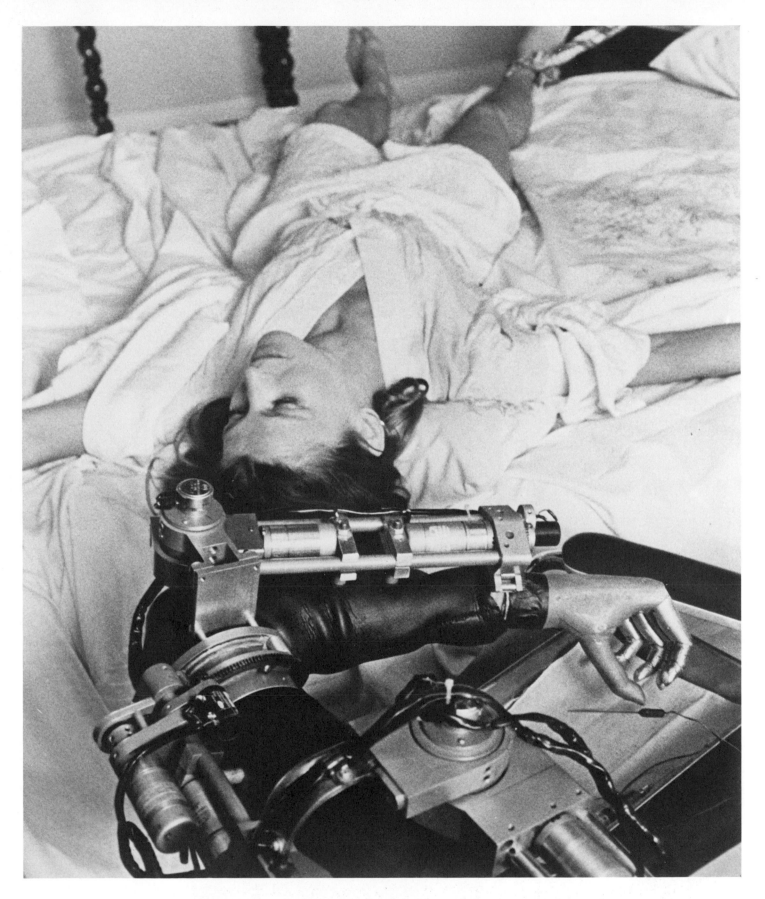

Proteus, the computer with a personality, uses mechanical agents to trap Julie Christie in her own home, in *Demon Seed* (MGM, 1977).

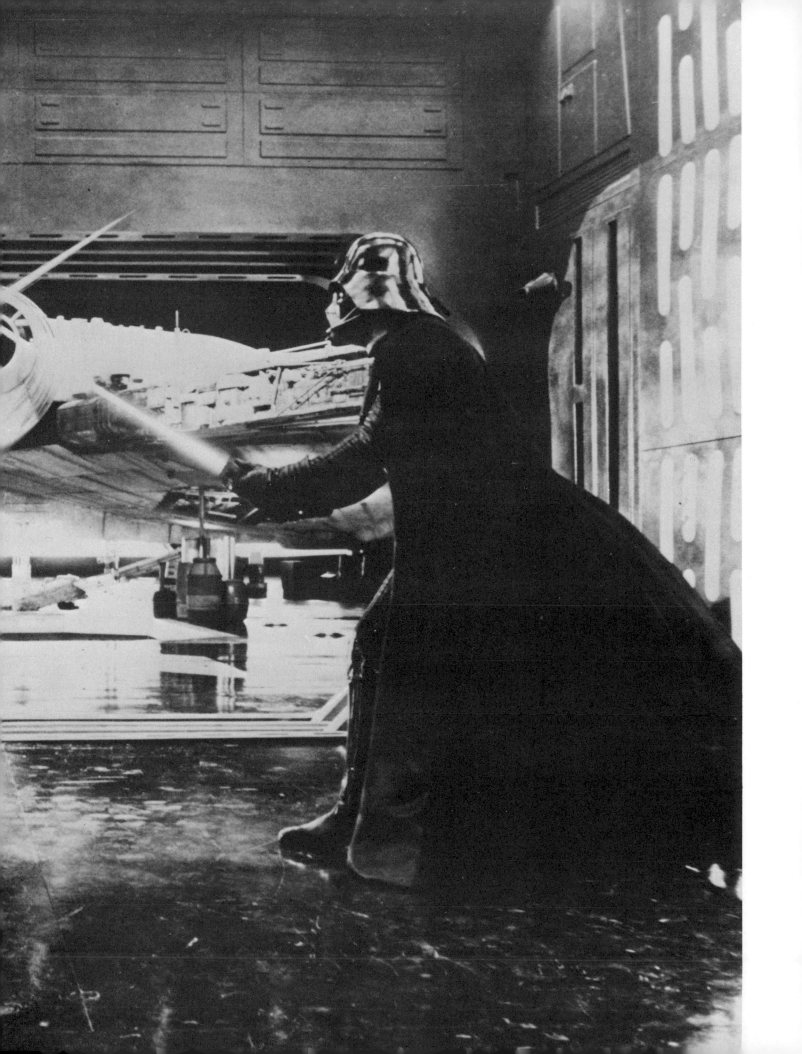

the night, and Luke sets off in pursuit the next morning. The robots and the boy are saved from the Sand People by Kenobi himself, and taken to his mountain hideaway. There, Kenobi listens to the tape, in which the Princess pleads for his help in delivering the vital information. Kenobi tells Luke a little about the boy's father, one of the Jedi knights who had helped preserve the Republic, and who had been treacherously betrayed by his friend, Lord Darth Vader (David Prowse). Vader had been one of Kenobi's star pupils (Kenobi himself is a Jedi), but had defected to the Empire years before.

Kenobi gives Luke his father's lightsword, a glowing laser that can cut through armor like a

(preceding pages)   Obi-Wan Kenobi (Alec Guinness) fights to the death with the evil Lord Darth Vader (David Prowse), one of his former pupils; in the background is Han Solo's ship, the "Millenium Falcon."—*Star Wars* (Twentieth Century-Fox, 1977).

(below)   Two of the Jawas, miniature scavengers on Tatooine, the desert planet where Luke Skywalker lives.—*Star Wars*.

(right)   An Imperial storm trooper, from *Star Wars* (1977).

knife through cheese. The old warrior tells Luke that he must respond to the Princess's demands, and he urges Luke to follow him. But Luke has other responsibilities, and returns briefly to his farm. In his absence, Imperial troops looking for the robots have slaughtered his family, and destroyed his homestead. With the two robots in tow, Luke and "Ben" (as Kenobi calls himself) head for the spaceport, where they engage pirate Captain Han Solo (Harrison Ford), and his fast freighter, the "Millenium Falcon." Solo's co-pilot is Chewbacca, a hundred-year-old giant Wookie (a cross between an ape and a bear) who speaks in grunts, howls, and groans. Their target is Alderaan, where forces sympathetic to the rebels can be contacted.

But the Empire is there before them, with the Dark Star now activated, and the Princess a prisoner in its depths. Grand Moff Tarkin (Peter Cushing) tells the Princess that he will destroy Alderaan unless she gives him the location of the rebel base; when she seems to relent, he orders it destroyed anyway, as an example of the Empire's power. Shortly thereafter, Solo breaks through from hyperspace, but all that remains of the planet are chunks of stone. The "Falcon" is captued by the Dark Star's tractor beam, and appears lost. But Solo has several escape holds

C3PO is confronted by the storm troopers.—*Star Wars* (Twentieth Century-Fox, 1977).

ready for just such an occasion, and the four intrepid warriors hide out while the stormtroopers search the craft.

Kenobi must hunt for the controls to the tractor beam; meanwhile, Luke and Han search for the Princess, and rescue her from her cell. After several running battles, the two spacemen get back to the launching hold, where the robots are already waiting. Kenobi, however, has been stopped by Darth Vader; master and pupil fight to the death with lightswords. Suddenly, Luke spots the battle, and is running towards them when Kenobi grins, turns, and drops his sword, as the beam of his enemy slices through his now empty garments. The survivors rush to the ship, seal the locks, and blast into space again.

After nominal resistance from the Tie fighters sent after them by the metal planetoid, the "Falcon" breaks free, and heads for Yavin, the rebel headquarters. There, R2-D2's material is digested by the computers, and a plan to attack is formulated. The giant enemy planetoid has followed them to Yavin, and is already approaching the rebel base. The rebels' only hope is to fling an atom bomb down a narrow venilation shaft in the Dark Star, where it will explode and start a chain reaction that will utterly destroy the villains. Luke himself pilots one of the small fighters attacking the Star. Darth Vader commands the fleet of fighters which swarm up in defense of the globe.

Barbara Carrera stars as Maria, the puma girl, in American International's remake of *The Island of Dr. Moreau* (1977).

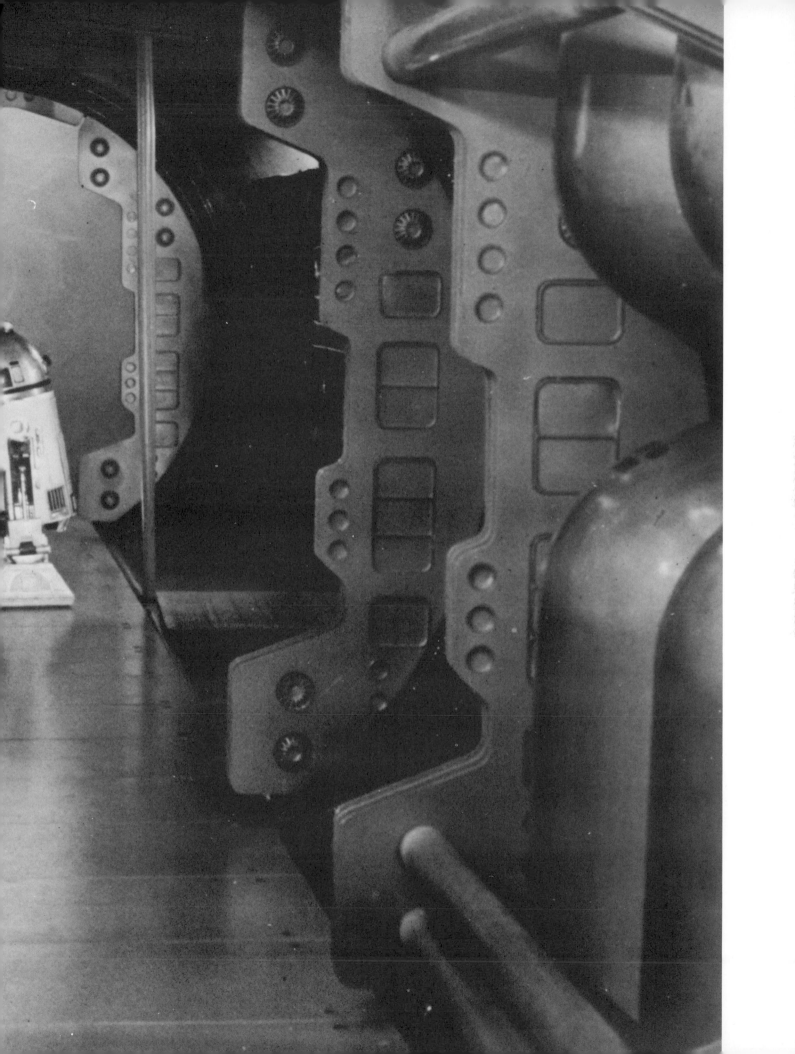

One after another, Luke's fellow fighters go down beneath the enemy's guns, as their bomb runs fail; finally, it's Luke's own turn. Trusting to the power of the Force, the mysterious energy behind the Jedi knights, Luke drops his bomb. His aim is true, and the Dark Star is destroyed. Back on Yavin, Princess Leia decorates Luke, Han, and Chewbacca for their services to the Republic. Vader, however, has escaped, and will undoubtedly be back to fight a second time. And so, of course, will the rest of the stars, since all of them were signed up for three movies.

Star Wars has already proved so successful that sequels seem certain. Its effects are being felt in other ways, too. Soon after **Star Wars** was released, Paramount announced a revival of the **Star Trek** television series, beginning in 1978. Other science fiction television and motion picture projects have reputedly been inaugurated directly as a result of this one example. The more important effects will be long term. **Star Wars** has set a new plateau of technical excellence that succeeding films will have to meet or exceed. Audiences will never again be satisfied with anything less. And if **Star Wars** becomes one of the ten top grossing films in the history of the industry, as it appears likely, there'll be no turning back.

Star Wars is, without a doubt, the first fully-realized science fiction movie ever made, the first film to make space travel seem the thing of wonder we always knew it was. The glory of the stars, the conquering of new worlds and vast interstellar spaces, communication with alien species, have all finally been brought to the screen. The only new developments can be those of character and plot. Eventually, of course, better movies will be made, as they always have been. Spielberg's new film, **Close Encounters of the Third Kind**, due to be released in late 1977, is reputedly very good. But **Star Wars** is destined to occupy a special niche in the history of the film: it will still be entertaining crowds fifty years from now. And fifty years from now, what else will we be watching? The marvel of tomorrow is that there are always things to come.

(preceding pages)   Princess Leia Organa (Carrie Fisher) transfers the blueprints of the ''Dark Star'' to R2-D2, as her space craft is captured by Imperials.—*Star Wars* (1977).

BIBLIOGRAPHY

Adler, Alan, ed. *Science Fiction and Horror Movie Posters in Full Color*. New York, Dover, 1977.

Agel, Jerome. *The Making of Kubrick's 2001*. New York, Signet, 1970.

Amelio, Ralph, J. *The Filmic Moment: Teaching American Genre Film Through Extracts*. Dayton, Pflaum, 1975.

_____. *HAL in the Classroom: Science Fiction Films*. Dayton, Pflaum, 1974.

Amis, Kingley. *New Maps of Hell*. New York, Harcourt Brace Jovanovich, 1960.

Annan, David. *Ape: Monster of the Movies*. London, Lorrimer, 1975.

_____. *Catastrophe: The End of the Cinema?* London, Lorrimer, 1975.

_____. *Cinefantastic: Beyond the Dream Machine*. London, Lorrimer, 1974.

_____. *Robot: The Mechanical Monster*. London, Lorrimer, 1976.

Atkins, Thomas R., ed. *Science Fiction Films*. New York, Monarch Press, 1976.

Barbour, Alan G. *Cliffhanger: A Pictorial History of the Motion Picture Serial*. New York, A & W Publishers, 1977.

Baxter, John. *Science Fiction in the Cinema*. London and New York, Tantivy Press/A. S. Barnes, 1974 (second edition, revised).

Boullet, Jean. *La Belle et la Bete*. Paris, Le Terrain Vague, 1958.

Braudy, Leo. *Jean Renoir: The World of His Films*. New York, Doubleday, 1972.

Bretnor, Reginald, ed. *Modern Science Fiction: Its Meaning and Its Future*. New York, Coward-Mc-Cann, 1953.

_____. *Science Fiction, Today and Tomorrow*. New York, Harper's, 1974.

Brosnan, John. *Movie Magic: The Story of Special Effects in the Cinema*. New York, St. Martin's Press, 1974.

Carrell, Christopher, ed. *Beyond This Horizon: An Anthology of Science Fact and Science Fiction*. Sunderland, England, Coelfrith Press, 1973.

Clarens, Carlos. *An Illustrated History of the Horror Film*. New York, Putnam's, 1967.

Dowdy, Andrew. *The Films of the Fifties: The American State of Mind*. New York, William Morrow, 1975.

Edelson, Edward. *Visions of Tomorrow: Great Science Fiction from the Movies*. New York, Doubleday, 1975.

Geduld, Carolyn. *Filmguide to 2001: A Space Odyssey*. Bloomington, Indiana State Press, 1973.

Gerani, Gary with Schulman, Paul H. *Fantastic Television*. New York, Harmony Books, 1977.

Gifford, Denis. *Science Fiction Film*. London and New York, Studio Vista/Dutton, 1971.

Goddard, Jean-Luc. *Alphaville*. London, Lorrimer, 1966.

Goldner, Orville and Turner, George E. *The Making of King Kong*. New York and London, A. S. Barnes/Tantivy Press, 1975.

Gottesman, Ronald and Geduld, Harry, eds. *The Girl in the Hairy Paw: King Kong as Myth, Movie, and Monster*. New York, Avon, 1976.

Hammond, Paul. *Marvellous Melies*. New York, St. Martin's Press, 1975.

Jensen, Paul M. *The Cinema of Fritz Lang*. New York and London, A. S. Barnes/A. Zwemmer, 1969.

Johnson, Wiliam, ed. *Focus on the Science Fiction Film*. Englewood Cliffs, Prentice-Hall, 1972.

Kagan, Norman. *The Cinema of Stanley Kubrick*. New York, Holt, Rinehart and Winston, 1972.

Kaminsky, Stuart M. *American Film Genres: Approaches to a Critical Theory of Popular Film*. Dayton, Pflaum, 1974.

Kracauer, Siegfried. *From Caligari to Hitler: A Psychological History of the German Film*. Princeton, Princeton University Press, 1947.

Kubrick, Stanley. *Stanley Kubrick's Clockwork Orange*. New York, Abelard-Schuman, 1972.

Laclos, Michel. *Le Fantastique au Cinema*. Paris, Jean-Jacques Pauvert, 1958.

Lang, Fritz. *Metropolis*. London, Lorrimer, 1973.

Lee, Walter. *Reference Guide to Fantastic Films: Science Fiction, Fantasy & Horror*. Los Angeles, Chelsea-Lee Books, 1972/1973/1974 (3 vols.).

Manvell, Roger and Fraenkel, Heinrich. *The German Cinema*. New York, Praeger, 1971.

Menville, Douglas. *A Historical and Critical Survey of the Science Fiction Film*. New York, Arno Press, 1975.

Pascall, Jeremy. *The King Kong Story*. London, Phoebus, 1976.

Phillips, Gene D. *Stanley Kubrick: A Film Odyssey*. New York, Popular Library, 1975.

Rovin, Jeff. *From Jules Verne to Star Trek*. New York, Drake, 1977.

_____. *A Pictorial History of Science Fiction Films*. Secaucus, Citadel Press, 1975.

Sadoul, Georges. *Georges Melies*. Paris, Editions Seghers, 1961.

Scholes, Robert and Rabkin, Eric C. *Science Fiction: History/Science/Vision*. New York, Oxford University Press, 1977.

Science Fiction Films from 1895 to 1930. London, British Film Institute, 1966.

Siclier, Jacques and Labarthe, Andre S. *Images de la Science-Fiction*. Paris, Les Editions du Cerf, 1958.

Steinbrunner, Chris and Goldblatt, Burt. *Cinema of the Fantastic*. New York, Saturday Review Press, 1972.

Sternberg, Jacques. *Une Succursale du Fantastique Nommee Science-Fiction*. Paris, Le Terrain Vague, 1958.

Strick, Philip. *Science Fiction Movies*. London, Octopus Books, 1976.

Tyler, Parker. *The Shadow of an Airplane Climbs the Empire State Building: A World Theory of Film*. New York, Doubleday, 1972.

Walker, Alexander. *Stanley Kubrick Directs*. New York, Harcourt Brace Jovanovich, 1971.

Wells, H. G. *The King Who Was a King: The Book of a Film*. London, Ernest Benn, 1929.

_____. Wells, H. G. *Things to Come: A Film by H. G. Wells*. New York, Macmillan, 1935.

_____. *The Time Machine/The War of the Worlds: A Critical Edition*. Edited by Frank D. McConnell. New York, Oxford University Press, 1977.

Will, David and Willemen, Paul, eds. *Roger Corman: The Millenic Vision*. Cambridge, Edinburgh Film Festival '70, n.d. (c. 1970).

Williamson, J. E. *Twenty Years Under the Sea*. New

York, Hale, Cushman, and Flint, 1936.
Willis, Donald C. *Horror and Science Fiction Films: A Checklist*. Metuchen, Scarecrow Press, 1972.

MAGAZINES

Castel of Frankenstein. 1962-1975.
Cinefantastique. 1970-
Classic Video Super Hits. Vol. 2, No. 1, April, 1977. (Special issue on SF films).
Famous Fantasy Films. 1966.
Famous Monsters of Filmland. 1958-
The Film Journal. No. 6, 1974. (Special issue on ''The Science Fiction Film Image'').
Kaleidoscope. Vol. 2, No. 2, 1966.
King of the Monsters. 1977- (Devoted to *King Kong* and other fantasy and SF films).
Kong. 1976.

Midi-Minuit Fantastique. 1962-1970.
The Mole People. 1964.
The Monster Times (tabloid newspaper). 1972-1976.
Monsters of the Movies. 1974-1975.
Movie Action Magazine. Vol. 1, No. 3, January, 1936. (Novelization of *The Invisible Ray*).
Phobos. 1977-
Photoplay Studies. Vol. 2, No. 4, April, 1936. (*Things to Come*).
Science Fiction Illustrated. 1977-
Screen Thrills Illustrated. 1962-1965.
Serial Quarterly. Vol. 2, No. 2, April-June, 1967. (*Buck Rogers* and *The Mysterious Island*).
Spacemen. 1961-1964.
Starlog. 1976-
Starlog Photo Guidebook. Vol. 1, No. 1, 1977. (Spaceships).
Ultra Ciencia. 1963-?

INDEX

212